heartsongs

heartsongs

Readings for Weddings

Collected by

Pinky Agnew

RANDOM HOUSE
NEW ZEALAND

DEDICATION

To my second husband, wherever he may be.

National Library of New Zealand Cataloguing-in-Publication Data

Heart songs: readings for weddings / Pinky Agnew (editor).
Includes index.
ISBN 1-86941-636-8
1. Love in literature. 2. Love poetry. 3. Marriage customs and rites.
I. Agnew, Pinky.
808.803543–dc 22

A RANDOM HOUSE BOOK
published by
Random House New Zealand
18 Poland Road, Glenfield, Auckland, New Zealand
www.randomhouse.co.nz

First published 2004

ISBN 1 86941 636 8

Text and cover design: Christine Hansen
Printed in China

Contents

THANKS

I thank all my friends and family for their patience and encouragement as I have worked on this book.

My heartfelt thanks to my greatest supporters — Kate Camp, friend, mentor, poet and girl next door; Belinda Kitchin whose idea this was; my patient editor Jenny Hellen; and Suzanne Kendrick who helped me find her. For help, encouragement and advice, I am grateful to Jane Westaway, Harry Ricketts, Kim Griggs, Margaret Agnew, Chris O'Kane, Hermione March, Nicola Edmonds, Roger Boyd, Rick Gekoski, Maria Champion-Forster and Bill Forster. Thanks also to Michael Moynahan, Sarah Ell and Sarah Thornton at Random House, and to Christine Hansen for her luscious design and heart photos.

Thanks also to the hundreds of couples who have shared their love stories with me, especially Celia West, my guardian angel, and Paul Forrest.

Thanks to Keri Hulme for inspiring the lovely title of this book, which comes from her poem 'Winesong 15' (see page 97 for a reading from this poem).

Finally, thanks for everything to my mother Jean Takacs, who has racked up fifty-six years on her marriage-ometer — thirty-six years with my late father Norman Agnew, and twenty years with my stepfather John Takacs.

I was sitting on a plane. The cabin attendant leaned across my two neighbours, and said in a cheerful Irish brogue, 'Ms Agnew, isn't it?'

'Yes,' I replied.

'Do you remember me?' he asked. 'You married me last year!' Light dawned. 'Oh of course, it's Michael, isn't it?'

'It is', he replied. 'You're good to remember. There must have been so many.' By now we had the interest not only of my seat-mates, but also of the passengers in the rows behind and in front of us. Realising they may have taken me for a serial bride, I made a general announcement. 'I'm a marriage celebrant. I married Michael . . . to someone else.'

I became a marriage celebrant in 1996 to add another source of income to my sometimes uncertain career as a comedian. I could not have guessed then how it would transform my life, and change my mind about love and relationships. I fell in love with the job.

As a celebrant, I become involved with a couple at an emotional high-point in their relationship. One of my brides, a midwife, said our jobs were similar. 'We're both with a couple at such an intimate and amazing time in their lives. Then we never see them again!'

Getting married is one of those life-steps that couples have always taken. For the modern couple, the steps themselves haven't changed, but the order in which they occur has. Instead of marrying at the start, couples often live together, buy a house, have children, and then marry.

So if couples have already taken those steps, and there are few legal advantages to marrying, why marry at all? It's a question I ask every couple during our first interview.

For most couples, the element of public declaration is important. 'It's an opportunity to declare our love and commitment publicly to our friends and families' is a pretty common comment.

Social pressure is sometimes a factor. For couples who have grown up in conservative families, marrying can be a way of fitting in, and of their partners being more greatly accepted into the family circle. Marriage is also seen as a comfortable social shorthand for 'This is the person I want to share my life and bills with and have children with. Please acknowledge them accordingly.'

Although some couples already have children from their current or past relationships, wanting to have children is still a reason to marry. 'We want our children to know that their Mum and Dad are in a committed relationship' is a typical feeling.

But at the heart of most weddings is the desire for the partners to make a declaration to each other; a commitment that they're in the relationship for the long haul. Marriage gives the relationship a sense of security, an emotional anchor.

Marriage laws have been considerably relaxed in New Zealand, although we still await the legalisation of same-sex marriages. Like many celebrants, I have conducted commitment ceremonies for gay couples. One couple had been together for ten years. When I asked them why they chose to have this ceremony, one said it was prompted by a visit to her partner's mother: 'All those photos on Nana's wall, and not one of us.' Getting married can be a declaration to the world, as well as to each other.

In New Zealand it is possible to marry at any type of venue, indoors or outdoors, at any time of day. The only legal requirements of the ceremony are that the couple should register their intent with Births, Death and Marriages at least three days beforehand, satisfying them that the marriage is bona fide; and that they exchange their vows before two witnesses and a duly appointed marriage celebrant, who declares them married and supervises the signing of the documents. Other countries have much stricter laws about where and when ceremonies may take place, and the words used.

This means couples who marry in New Zealand are able to have ceremonies that are personal and unique, in a venue that is right for their needs. For some, that is in a church, with a traditional religious service, but the majority marrying in New Zealand today choose a civil ceremony. This may be conducted by a registrar at the Registry Office, but most choose a local celebrant, and a venue that feels right for them.

Which is where I come in. As a celebrant, I have three primary responsibilities. One responsibility is legal. As a registered civil celebrant, I make sure that all documents are accurate and are correctly processed, and that the legal requirements of the ceremony are fulfilled.

Another responsibility is to conduct the ceremony exactly as the couple wishes. Everyone loves a wedding, and many people believe they know how things should be done. Weddings can be hijacked by all sorts of people — mothers, sisters, bridesmaids, photographers, even celebrants — who think they know what should be said, and who should do what, standing or sitting where. My job is to make sure that the couple's wedding is exactly that: *their* wedding, done *their* way.

The greatest responsibility I take on is to write a ceremony for the couple, reflecting their unique personalities, their tastes, traditions, and cultures. I do this after spending time with them, asking questions about themselves and their relationship. I encourage couples to think deeply about their ceremony, and to identify what it is that they really want to say. A big part of my job is to interpret this for them, and to craft their words and feelings into a wedding ceremony.

If a wedding ceremony addressed only the legal requirements, it would be over in three minutes. Most people want a ceremony that is much more personal, but have no idea where to start. Drawing out their feelings and creating a unique ceremony for each couple is a wonderful process for me.

I love hearing each member of the couple talk about the other. I remember one groom-to-be, a weather-beaten Scot, thought deeply when I asked him what he loved about his fiancée. Finally he spoke: 'Well, ya naw, my heart just pumps custard fur this woman.'

Another way people choose to make their ceremony unique is to have readings. When I make my first visit to see a couple, I lug with me a big ring-binder bulging with copies of poems, Bible readings and prose pieces that I have collected over the years. Couples love browsing through the collection, picking out readings for their wedding.

At weddings, I have seen readings tickle funny bones and bring tears to eyes. Readings can be a way of saying something that the couple may not have words for. Asking a particular person to read a special piece can also be a way of including someone who is special to the couple but who is not a part of the wedding party. In the case of religious readings or prayers, it can be a way of honouring the beliefs of family.

Sometimes, friends or family members, or even the couple themselves, write something especially for the wedding day, which adds a special emotional dimension.

The selection I have chosen for this book covers a wide range of styles. Wherever possible I have attributed sources. However, some have only survived as legacies of that most prolific writer, Anonymous. If you do pass readings on to others, please, wherever possible, add the author's name. They deserve the acknowledgement for their beautiful words.

I have also included quotations to use in the wedding ceremony, in speeches or toasts, or on wedding invitations and thank-you notes. They can also be used in cards sent to an engaged or married couple.

During my time as a celebrant I have listened to hundreds of stories about love, relationships and commitment from the couples I have worked with. I have witnessed the healing power of love, that majestic emotion that beats in the heart of the motor mechanic, the managing director, the manicurist. Being with people at this joyous time of their lives, and hearing their stories, has changed forever my own feelings about love.

I have also seen the value of commitment in a relationship. Whatever it is that we do — whether it is sport or work or art or music — it is better if we do it with commitment. And so it is with relationships.

An event like the death of someone close, an illness, the birth of a child, or an accident can sometimes be a catalyst for a couple deciding to make the commitment of marriage. One couple I worked with were rock climbing together in Asia. He slipped, and she grasped his hand with all her strength as she lay on her stomach on a tiny ledge, the sharp rock sawing at her fingers with every movement. She held him for what seemed like an eternity until he was able to swing himself up to safety. 'Having come so close to losing each other, we knew we wanted to be together forever,' they said. Or, as Shakespeare wrote, 'Now join your hands, and with your hands, your hearts.'

Tips for readings at the wedding ceremony

When asking someone to read at your ceremony, choose the reading yourselves, or give the reader a selection to choose from. Some readings may not feel right for you.

When asking someone to read at a wedding, send the reading to them as far in advance as possible. This gives them time to familiarise themselves with it.

If you have been asked to read something at a wedding, practice reading it aloud several times. This will make your reading flow better on the day, and help reduce nerves.

Often there will not be a microphone, so try to project your voice to the person furthest away from you, and speak slowly.

Make sure your reading is easy to read. If necessary, re-type it using a larger font and double spacing. If you worry that your hands may shake, paste it onto card, or read it straight from this book!

Chapter One

CLASSICAL LOVE

Now join your hands,
and with your hands,
your hearts.

WILLIAM SHAKESPEARE
KING HENRY VI PART III

Chapter One

CLASSICAL LOVE

Shakespeare wrote so beautifully and acutely of love that no matter how the language has changed, we know that love hasn't.

One wedding I officiated at had guests who were actors. Hearing a skilled performer read Shakespeare's 'Sonnet 116', which begins 'Let me not to the marriage of true minds/Admit impediments', I realised I had never really understood the words before, because I had never heard them read with such meaning.

Reading classic words aloud is always a challenge. If you have been asked to read something like this at a wedding, practise reading it aloud beforehand. Read it closely to yourself, trying to understand each line, so you can read with good expression.

One couple used such readings in their vows. She used the first part of Elizabeth Barrett Browning's 'Sonnets From The Portuguese XLIII':
> 'How do I love thee? Let me count the ways.
> I love thee to the depth and breadth and height
> My soul can reach, when feeling out of sight
> For the end of being and ideal grace.'

He made his vows the second part of the same poem:
> 'I love thee freely, as men strive for right;
> I love thee purely, as they turn from praise.
> I love thee with the passion put to use
> In my old griefs, and with my childhood's faith.
> I love thee with a love I seemed to lose
> With my lost saints — I love thee with the breath,
> Smile, tears, of all of my life! — and if God choose,
> I shall but love thee better after death.'

Another couple had met when they acted in their school play, Shakespeare's *Hamlet*. We closed the ceremony with this quote from the play:

> 'Doubt that the stars are fire;
> Doubt that the sun doth move;
> Doubt truth to be a liar;
> But never doubt that I love.'

These are beautiful works that have stood the test of time. Even though we may have heard them many times, we never tire of them.

If thou must love me, let it be for nought
Except for love's sake only. Do not say,
'I love her for her smile — her look — her way
Of speaking gently, — for a trick of thought
That falls in well with mine, and certes brought
A sense of pleasant ease on such a day' —
For these things in themselves, Beloved, may
Be changed, or change for thee, — and love, so wrought,
May be unwrought so. Neither love me for
Thine own dear pity's wiping my cheeks dry,
Since one might forget to weep, who bore
Thy comfort long, and lose thy love thereby!
But love me for love's sake, that evermore
Thou may'st love on, through love's eternity.

ELIZABETH BARRETT BROWNING (1806-1861)

When our two souls stand up erect and strong,
Face to face, silent, drawing nigh and nigher,
Until the lengthening wings break into fire
At either curved point, — what bitter wrong
Can earth do to us, that we should not long
Be there contented? Think. In mounting higher,
The angels would press on us and aspire
To drop some golden orb of perfect song
Into our deep, dear silence. Let us stay
Rather on earth, Beloved, — where the unfit
Contrarious moods of men recoil away
And isolate pure spirits, and permit
A place to stand and love in for a day,
With darkness and the death-hour rounding it.

ELIZABETH BARRETT BROWNING (1806-1861)

How do I love thee? Let me count the ways.
I love thee to the depth and breadth and height
My soul can reach, when feeling out of sight
For the ends of Being and ideal Grace.
I love thee to the level of everyday's
Most quiet need, by sun and candlelight.
I love thee freely, as men strive for Right;
I love thee purely, as they turn from Praise.
I love thee with the passion put to use
In my old griefs, and with my childhood's faith.
I love thee with a love I seemed to lose
With my lost saints — I love thee with the breath,
Smiles, tears, of all of my life! — and if God choose,
I shall but love thee better after death.

ELIZABETH BARRETT BROWNING (1806-1861)

If ever two were one, then surely we.
If ever man were loved by wife, then thee;
If ever wife was happy in a man,
Compare with me, ye women, if you can
I prize thy love more than whole mines of gold.
Or all the riches that the East doth hold.
My love is such that rivers cannot quench,
Nor ought but love from thee, give recompense.
Thy love is such I can no way repay,
The heavens reward thee manifold, I pray,
Then while we live, in love let's so persevere
That when we live no more, we may live ever.

ANNE BRADSTREET (1612-1672)

Grow old along with me!
The best is yet to be,
The last of life, for which the first was made:
Our times are in his hand
Who saith, 'A whole I planned,
Youth shows but half; trust God: see all, nor be afraid!'

ROBERT BROWNING (1812-1889)

A RED, RED ROSE

O my Luve's like a red, red rose,
That's newly sprung in June;
O my Luve's like the melodie
That's sweetly played in tune.

As fair art thou, my bonnie lass,
So deep in luve am I;
And I will love thee still, my Dear,
Till a' the seas gang dry.

Till a' the seas gang dry, my Dear,
And the rocks melt wi' the sun;
I will love thee still my Dear,
While the sands o' life shall run.

And fare thee weel, my only Luve!
And fare thee weel, a while!
And I will come again, my Luve,
Tho' it were ten thousand mile!

ROBERT BURNS (1759-1796)

Wild nights — Wild nights!
Were I with thee,
Wild nights should be
Our luxury!

Futile — the Winds —
To a Heart in port —
Done with the Compass —
Done with the Chart!

Rowing in Eden —
Ah, the Sea!
Might I but moor — Tonight —
In Thee!

EMILY DICKINSON (1830-1886)

No speed of wind or water rushing by
But you have speed far greater. You can climb
Back up a stream of radiance to the sky,
And back through history up the stream of time.
And you were given this swiftness, not for haste
Nor chiefly that you may go where you will,
But in the rush of everything to waste,
That you may have the power of standing still —
Off any still or moving thing you say.
Two such as you with such a master speed
Cannot be parted nor be swept away
From one another once you are agreed
That life is only life forevermore
Together wing to wing and oar to oar.

ROBERT FROST (1874-1963)

Julia, I bring
To thee this Ring.
Made for thy finger fit;
To shew by this,
That our love is
(Or sho'd be) like to it.

Close though it be,
The joynt is free:
So when Love's yoke is on,
It must not gall,
Or fret at all
With hard oppression.

But it must play
Still either way;
And be, too, such a yoke,
As not too wide,
To over-slide;
Or be so strait to choak.

So we, who beare,
The beame, must reare
Our selves to such a height:
As that the stay
Of either may
Create the burden light.

And as this round
Is no where found
To flaw, or else to sever:
So let our love
As endless prove;
And pure as Gold for ever.

ROBERT HERRICK (1591-1624)

And is it night? Are they thine eyes that shine?
Are we alone and here and here alone?
May I come near, may I but touch thy shrine?
Is jealousy asleep, and is he gone?
O Gods, no more, silence my lips with thine,
Lips, kisses, joys, hap, blessings most divine.

O come my dear, our griefs are turned to night,
And night to joys, night blinds pale Envy's eyes,
Silence and sleep prepare our delight,
O cease we then our woes, our griefs, our cries,
O vanish words, words do but passions move,
O dearest life, joys sweet, O sweetest love.

ROBERT JONES (c. 1609)

Love feels no burden,
thinks nothing of trouble,
attempts what is above its strength,
pleads no excuse of impossibility . . .
It is therefore able to undertake all things,
and it completes many things,
and warrants them to take effect,
where he who does not love would faint and lie down.
Love is watchful and sleeping, slumbereth not.
Though weary, it is not tired;
though pressed, it is not straitened;
though alarmed, it is not confounded.

THOMAS À KEMPIS (1379-1471)

Come live with me and be my Love,
And we will all the pleasures prove
That valleys, groves, hills and fields,
Woods, or steepy mountain yields.

And we will sit upon the rocks
Seeing shepherds feed their flocks,
By shallow rivers to whose falls
Melodious birds sing madrigals.

There will I make thee beds of roses
And a thousand fragrant posies,
A cap of flowers, and a kirtle
Embroidered all with leaves of myrtle;

A gown made of the finest wool
Which from our pretty lambs we pull;
Fair linèd slippers for the cold,
With buckles of the purest gold;

A belt of straw and ivy buds,
With coral clasps and amber studs:
And if these pleasures may thee move,
Come live with me, and be my love.

The shepherd's swains shall dance and sing
For thy delight each May morning:
If these delights thy mind may move,
Then live with me and be my Love.

CHRISTOPHER MARLOWE (1564-1593)

O lay thy hand in mine, dear!
We're growing old, we're growing old;
But Time hath brought no sign, dear,
That hearts grow cold, that hearts grow cold,
'Tis long, long since our new love
Made life divine, made life divine;
But age enricheth true love,
Like noble wine, like noble wine.

GERALD MASSEY (1828-1907)

Never marry but for love; but see that thou lovest what is lovely. He that minds a body and not a soul has not the better part of that relationship, and will consequently lack the noblest comfort of a married life.

Between a man and his wife nothing ought to rule but love. As love ought to bring them together, so it is the best way to keep them well together.

A husband and wife that love one another show their children that they should do so too. Others visibly lose their authority in their families by their contempt of one another, and teach their children to be unnatural by their own examples.

Let not enjoyment lessen, but augment, affection; it being the basest of passions to like when we have not, what we slight when we possess.

Here it is we ought to search out our pleasure, where the field is large and full of variety, and of an enduring nature; sickness, poverty or disgrace being not able to shake it because it is not under the moving influences of worldly contingencies.

Nothing can be more entire and without reserve; nothing more zealous, affectionate and sincere; nothing more contented than such a couple, nor greater temporal felicity than to be one of them.

WILLIAM PENN (1644-1718)

No sooner met but they looked;
No sooner looked but they loved;
No sooner loved but they sighed;
No sooner sighed but they asked one another the reason;
No sooner knew the reason but they sought the remedy.

WILLIAM SHAKESPEARE (1564-1616)

from HAMLET

Doubt that the stars are fire;
Doubt that the sun doth move;
Doubt truth to be a liar;
But never doubt that I love.

WILLIAM SHAKESPEARE (1564-1616)

Shall I compare thee to a summer's day?
Thou art more lovely and more temperate:
Rough winds do shake the darling buds of May,
And summer's lease hath all too short a date:
Sometime too hot the eye of heaven shines,
And often is his gold complexion dimm'd,
And every fair from fair sometime declines,
By chance or nature's changing course untrimm'd;
But thy eternal summer shall not fade,
Nor lose possession of that fair thou owest,
Nor shall death brag thou wandrest in his shade,
When in eternal lines to time thou growest;
So long as men can breathe or eyes can see,
So long lives this, and this gives life to thee.

WILLIAM SHAKESPEARE (1564-1616)

When in disgrace with Fortune and men's eyes,
I all alone beweep my outcast state,
And trouble deaf heaven with my bootless cries,
And look upon myself and curse my fate,
Wishing me like to one more rich in hope,
Featured like him, like him with friends possessed,
Desiring this man's art and that man's scope,
With what I most enjoy contented least;
Yet in these thoughts myself almost despising
Haply I think on thee, and then my state,
Like to the lark at break of day arising
From sullen earth, sings hymns at heaven's gate:
For thy sweet love remember'd such wealth brings
That then I scorn to change my state with Kings.

WILLIAM SHAKESPEARE (1564-1616)

To me fair friend you never can be old,
For as you were when first your eye I eyed,
Such seems your beauty still: three winters cold,
Have from the forests shook three summers' pride,
Three beauteous springs to yellow autumn turned,
In process of the seasons have I seen,
Three April perfumes in three hot Junes burned,
Since first I saw you fresh which yet are green.
Ah yet doth beauty like a dial hand,
Steal from his figure, and no pace perceived,
So your sweet hue, which methinks still doth stand
Hath motion, and mine eye may be deceived.
For fear of which, hear this thou age unbred,
Ere you were born was beauty's summer dead.

WILLIAM SHAKESPEARE (1564-1616)

Let me not to the marriage of true minds
Admit impediments. Love is not love
Which alters when it alteration finds,
Or bends with the remover to remove.
O, no! It is an ever-fixed mark,
That looks on tempests and is never shaken;
It is the star to every wand'ring bark;
Whose worth's unknown, although his height be taken.
Love's not Time's fool, though rosy lips and cheeks
Within his bending sickle's compass come;
Love alters not with his brief hours and weeks,
But bears it out even to the edge of doom.
If this be error, and upon me proved,
I never writ, nor no man ever lov'd.

WILLIAM SHAKESPEARE (1564-1616)

The fountains mingle with the river
And the rivers with the ocean,
The winds of heaven mix for ever,
With a sweet emotion;
Nothing in the world is single,
All things by a law divine
In another's being mingle —
Why not I with thine?

See the mountains kiss high heaven,
And the waves clasp one another;
No sister-flower would be forgiven
If it disdain'd its brother:

And the sunlight clasps the earth,
And the moonbeams kiss the sea —
What are all these kissings worth,
If thou kiss not me?

PERCY BYSSHE SHELLEY (1792-1822)

My true love hath my heart, and I have his,
By just exchange one for another given:
I hold his deare, and mine he cannot misse,
There never was a better bargaine driven.
My true love hath my heart, and I have his.

His heart in me keepes him and me in one,
My heart in him his thoughts and senses guides;
He loves my heart, for once it was his owne,
I cherish his, because in me it bides.
My true love hath my heart and I have his.

SIR PHILIP SIDNEY (1554-1586)

Heart, are you great enough
For love that never tires?
O heart, are you great enough for love?
I have heard of thorns and briers.
Over the thorns and briers,
Over the meadows and stiles,
Over the world to the end of it
Flash for a million miles.

ALFRED, LORD TENNYSON (1809-1892)

A DRINKING SONG

Wine comes in at the mouth
And love comes in at the eye;
That's all we shall know for truth
Before we grow old and die.
I lift the glass to my mouth,
I look at you, and I sigh.

W.B. YEATS (1865-1939)

Had I the heavens' embroidered cloths,
Enwrought with golden and silver light,
The blue and the dim and the dark cloths
Of night and light and the half-light,
I would spread the cloths under your feet:
But I, being poor, have only my dreams;
I have spread my dreams under your feet;
Tread softly because you tread on my dreams.

W.B. YEATS (1865-1939)

Chapter Two

HOLY LOVE

Many waters cannot quench love,
neither can the floods drown it.

SONG OF SONGS, THE BIBLE

Where love is, no room is too
small.

TALMUD

Chapter Two

Most couples who choose a civil ceremony have no church ties and don't want a religious ceremony. Many do have spiritual beliefs of some kind though, and sometimes want to include a prayer or spiritual reading in the ceremony. I have conducted ceremonies where a Catholic priest, Buddhist monk or Presbyterian minister have given blessings and led prayers, and I have led prayers myself.

Having a religious reading can also be a way of honouring the beliefs of family members. A parent may be hurt that their child chooses not to marry in their church. Asking the parent to lead a prayer or read from the Bible can assuage these feelings. In this, as in every aspect of the ceremony, the couple should always make the decision themselves, and should never compromise their own beliefs.

One couple decided to honour the groom's Jewish heritage by marrying under a chuppah, a traditional canopy. He broke a glass under his heel, another Jewish wedding custom. The bride's Celtic background was acknowledged with an Irish drum accompanying her entrance to the room, and a Celtic prayer.

Another wedding had a beautiful Buddhist ritual. A golden cord was unravelled by a monk, who gave one end of it to the bride. The cord was then unwound and passed amongst the guests, finishing with the groom, who also held the bride's hand. Everyone there was linked by the golden cord, while the guests were asked to reflect on the loving life they wanted the couple to enjoy together, and their connection to them and to each other. Then the monk wound the cord back up, and after the ceremony he cut the cord into pieces. Each guest approached, and a piece of the cord was tied around their wrist. Many guests wore the cord until it disintegrated, and others kept it as a keepsake.

One couple wanted a pagan ceremony, in keeping with their beliefs in spirits of nature. The day before their outdoor wedding, using a compass, the three of us marked out the circle of stones in which the ceremony would take place. I arrived the next day to discover that a helpful groundsman had collected up all the stones to mow the area, and had put them in a neat pile. Another guest and I put them out again, without the help of a compass. I'm sure the great stone gods would have understood!

All Bible excerpts (unless stated) are from *The Holy Bible New Revised Standard Version* (Oxford University Press).

Let us pray.

God, bless the marriage of ___ _____ and _____ .

Together may they build a life where they know each other's strengths, nurture each other's talents, and support each other's needs.

May they work together, play together, laugh together, and dream together.

May they show others that, with love, life has hope, life has meaning, and life is good.

May they share values, share faith, share sorrow, share joy.

Witness their love, Lord, and help them make it deeper and stronger with time. For this is why we are born — to love and to be loved.

AMEN

PINKY AGNEW

May God grant _____ and _____ ,
enough love to give each other trust,
enough trust to give each other faith,
enough faith to give each other strength,
enough strength to give each other courage,
enough courage to give each other freedom,
and enough freedom to give each other love.

AMEN

PINKY AGNEW

All praise and blessing to you, God of love,
Creator of the universe,
Maker of man and woman in your likeness,
Source of blessing for married life.

All praise to you, for you have created
Courtship and marriage,
Joy and gladness,
feasting and laughter,
Pleasure and delight.

May your blessing come in full upon
_____ and _____ ,
May they know your presence in their joys and sorrows,
May they reach old age in the company of friends
And come at last to your eternal kingdom.

AMEN

ANGLICAN PRAYER

So the Lord God caused a deep sleep to fall upon the man, and he slept; then he took one of his ribs and closed up its place with flesh. And the rib that the Lord God had taken from the man he made into a woman and brought her to the man. Then the man said, 'This at last is bone of my bones and flesh of my flesh; this one shall be called Woman, for out of Man this one was taken.' Therefore a man leaves his father and his mother and clings to his wife, and they become one flesh.

KING JAMES VERSION

Intreat me not to leave thee,
or to return from following after thee;
for whither thou goest, I will go;
and whither thou lodgest, I will lodge;
thy people shall be my people, and thy God my God:
Where thou diest, will I die, and there will I be buried:
the Lord do so to me, and more also,
if ought but death part thee and me.

KING JAMES VERSION

For everything there is a season, and a time for every matter under heaven:
a time to be born, and a time to die;
a time to plant, and a time to pluck up what is planted;
a time to kill, and a time to heal;
a time to break down, and a time to build up;
a time to weep, and a time to laugh;
a time to mourn, and a time to dance;
a time to throw away stones, and a time to gather stones together;
a time to embrace, and a time to refrain from embracing;
a time to seek, and a time to lose;
a time to keep, and a time to throw away;
a time to tear, and a time to sew;
a time to keep silence, and a time to speak;
a time to love, and a time to hate;
a time for war, and a time for peace.

Two are better than one, because they have a good reward for their toil. For if
they fall, one will lift up the other, but woe to one who is alone and falls, and
does not have another to help. Again, if two lie together, they keep warm; but
how can one keep warm alone? Though one might prevail against another,
two will withstand one. A threefold cord is not quickly broken.

I am my beloved's,
and his desire is for me.
Come, my beloved,
let us go forth into the fields,
and lodge in the villages;
let us go out early to the vineyards,
and see whether the vines have budded,
whether the grape blossoms have opened
and the pomegranates are in bloom.
There I will give you my love.
The mandrakes give forth fragrance,
and over our doors are all the choice fruits,
new as well as old, which I have laid up for you,
O my beloved.

Set me as a seal upon your heart,
as a seal upon your arm;
for love is strong as death,
passion fierce as the grave.
Its flashes are flashes of fire,
a raging flame.
Many waters cannot quench love,
neither can floods drown it.
If one offered for love
all the wealth of his house,
it would be utterly scorned.

I will woo her, I will go with her into the wilderness and comfort her: there I
will restore her vineyards, turning the Vale of Trouble into the Gate of Hope,
and there she will answer as in her youth, when she came up out of Egypt. On
that day she shall call me 'My husband' . . .
Then I will make a covenant on behalf of Israel with the wild beasts, the birds
of the air, and the things that creep on the earth, and I will break bow and
sword and weapon of war and sweep them off the earth, so that all living
creatures may lie down without fear.
I will betroth you to myself forever, betroth you in lawful wedlock with
unfailing devotion and love; I will betroth you to myself to have and to hold . . .
I will answer for the heavens, and they will answer for the earth, and the earth
will answer for the corn, the new wine and the oil.

NEW ENGLISH BIBLE

Love is patient; love is kind; love is not envious or boastful or arrogant or rude. It does not insist on its own way; it is not irritable or resentful, it does not rejoice in wrongdoing, but rejoices in the truth. It bears all things, believes all things, hopes all things, endures all things.

And now faith, hope and love abide, these three; and the greatest of these is love.

God made woman from man's rib,
Not from his head . . .
That he should command her,
Nor from his feet . . .
That he should walk upon her,
But rather from his side . . .
To be his partner in life,
From under his arm . . .
To be protected by him,
And from near his heart . . .
To be loved by him.

AUTHOR UNKNOWN

We thank God, then, for the pleasures, joys and triumphs of marriage; for the cups of tea we bring each other, and the seedlings in the garden frame; for the domestic drama of meetings and partings, sickness and recovery; for the grace of occasional extravagance, flowers on birthdays and unexpected presents; for talk at evenings of the events of the day; for the ecstasy of caresses; for plans and projects, fun and struggle; praying that we may neither neglect nor undervalue these things, nor be tempted to think of them as self-contained and self-sufficient.

SOCIETY OF FRIENDS

6

Give joy to these lovers, as you gave joy to the first lovers in Eden.
Blessed is the One who brings happiness to the bride and groom.

7

Blessed is the One who makes joy and gladness, bride and bridegroom,
laughter and exultation, merriment and delight, love and friendship, peace and
companionship.

Soon may we hear in the cities of Judah and in the streets of Jerusalem the
voice of joy and the voice of gladness; the voice of the groom and the voice of
the bride; the delight of the couple under the canopy; the songs of the people
as they celebrate.

Blessed is the one who brings joy to the bride and groom.

TRADITIONAL JEWISH WEDDING BLESSING

Develop a love that is truly great, free from possessiveness,
a strong, clear love, not overwhelmed by desire,
a love that is joyful, and celebrates intimacy,
a love that is firm but not grasping,
unshakable but free,
hard and brilliant as a diamond, but not harsh,

helpful but not interfering,
giving more than taking,
dignified but not proud,
gentle but not weak,
refreshing and invigorating,
peaceful and settled.

Such a love leads one to the heights of clear, blissful awareness.

(ADAPTED FROM A BUDDHIST SUTRA)

My friend, I cannot answer when you ask me to explain
what has befallen me.
Love is transformed, renewed,
each moment.
He has dwelt in my eyes all the days of my life,
yet I am not sated with seeing.
My ears have heard his sweet voice in eternity,
and yet it is always new to them.
How many honeyed nights have I passed with him
in love's bliss, yet my body
wonders at his.
Through all the ages
he has been clasped to my breast,
yet my desire
never abates.
I have seen subtle people sunk in passion
but none came so close to the heart of the fire.

VIDYAPATI

Grant, O God/dess, thy Protection
And in Protection, Strength
And in Strength, Understanding
And in Understanding, Knowledge
And in Knowledge, the Knowledge of Justice
And in the Knowledge of Justice, the Love of it
And in the Love of it, The Love of all Existences
And in the Love of all Existences, the Love of the God/dess
    and all Goodness.

AUTHOR UNKNOWN

IRISH BLESSING

May the road rise to meet you,
And the sun stand at your shoulder.
May the wind be always at your back,
May the sun shine warm upon your face,
May the rain fall soft upon your fields.
And until we meet again,
May God hold you in the palm of His hand.

AMEN

AUTHOR UNKNOWN

CELTIC BLESSING

Goodness of sea be yours,
Goodness of earth be yours
Goodness of heaven.

Each day be joyous to you
No day be grievous to you.
Love of each face be yours

A bright flame before thee
A guiding star above thee
A smooth path below thee

Today, tonight and for evermore.

Deep peace of the running wave to you.
Deep peace of the flowing air to you.
Deep peace of the quiet earth to you.
Deep peace of the shining stars to you.
Deep peace of the Son of Peace to you.

ADAPTED FROM ANCIENT GAELIC RUNES

APACHE BLESSING

Now you will feel no rain, for each of you will be shelter for the other.
Now you will feel no cold, for each of you will be warmth to the other.
Now there will be no loneliness, for each of you will be companion to the
other.
Now you are two persons, but there is only one life before you.
May beauty surround you both in the journey ahead and through all the years.
May happiness be your companion and your days together be good and long
upon the earth.

Treat yourselves and each other with respect, and remind yourselves often of
what brought you together.
Give the highest priority to the tenderness, gentleness and kindness that your
connection deserves.
When frustration, difficulties and fear assail your relationship,
as they threaten all relationships at one time or another,
remember to focus on what is right between you, not only the part which
seems wrong.
In this way, you can ride out the storms when clouds hide the face of the sun in
your lives — remembering that even if you lose sight of it for a moment, the
sun is still there.
And if each of you takes responsibility for the quality of your life together,
it will be marked by abundance and delight.

AUTHOR UNKNOWN

God grant me the serenity to accept
the things I cannot change;
courage to change the things I can;
and wisdom to know the difference.

AMEN

REINHOLD NIEBUHR

Chapter Three

INSPIRATIONAL LOVE

Don't walk in front of me,
I may not follow.
Don't walk behind me,
I may not lead.
Just walk beside me
and be my friend forever.

ALBERT CAMUS

Chapter Three

INSPIRATIONAL LOVE

Many wedding readings have a spiritual or New Age flavour. In the 21st century, New Age now seems quaintly old fashioned. Some of these readings are recycled from my younger years, and were popular in the 1960s. No student flat was complete without a copy of the Desiderata on the wall. People are now rediscovering these poems and finding them inspirational.

Some couples have weddings that reflect pagan or other spiritual beliefs. One pair opted for a release of white doves after their vows. After a hot wait, the birds were too tired to leave their box, and had to be vigorously coaxed out. They flapped sluggishly to a nearby tree.

Another couple had a butterfly theme for their day. A large muslin container held twenty monarch butterflies, which obviously felt the cold, as they clung resolutely to the fabric and refused to be released. Our patience was rewarded as the butterflies warmed up and flew out, where they settled on the bride and some of the guests, making a beautiful sight.

Whatever inspires a couple, their ceremony should express their beliefs, and have rituals and readings that are meaningful to them.

ESKIMO LOVE SONG

You are my wife [husband]
My feet shall run because of you.
My feet, dance because of you.
My heart shall beat because of you.
My eyes, see because of you.
My mind, think because of you.
And I shall love because of you.

AUTHOR UNKNOWN

Fair is the white star of twilight,
and the sky clearer at the day's end;
But she is fairer, and she is dearer.
She, my heart's friend!

Far stars and fair in the skies bending,
Low stars of hearth fires and wood smoke ascending,
The meadow-lark's nested,
The night hawk is winging;
Home through the star-shine the hunter comes singing.

Fair is the white star of twilight,
And the moon roving
To the sky's end;
But she is fairer, better worth loving,
She, my heart's friend.

A SHOSHONE INDIAN LOVE SONG

To laugh is to risk appearing the fool.

To weep is to risk appearing sentimental.

To reach out to another is to risk involvement.

To expose feeling is to risk exposing your true self.

To place your ideas, your dreams before the crowd is to risk their loss.

To live is to risk dying.

To try is to risk failure.

But risk must be taken because the greatest hazard in life is to risk nothing.

The person who risks nothing, does nothing, has nothing, and is nothing.

You may avoid suffering and sorrow, but you simply cannot learn, feel, change, grow, love, live.

Chained by your certitudes you are a slave.

You have forfeited freedom.

Only a person who risks is free.

AUTHOR UNKNOWN

Look to this day,
For it is life, the very life of life.
In its brief course lie all the verities and realities
of your existence;
the bliss of growth,
the glory of action,
the splendour of beauty.

For yesterday is but a dream
and tomorrow is only a vision,
but today well-lived makes
every yesterday a dream of happiness
and every tomorrow a vision of hope.

Look well, therefore, to this day,
such is the salutation of the dawn.

When two people are at one in their inmost hearts, they shatter even the strength of iron or bronze.

And when two people understand each other in their inmost hearts, their words are sweet and strong like the fragrance of orchids.

Go placidly amidst the noise and haste, and remember
what peace there may be in silence. As far as possible,
without surrender, be on good terms with all persons.
Speak your truth quietly and clearly; and listen to others . . .

If you compare yourself with others, you may become
bitter or vain, for always there will be greater and lesser
persons than yourself. Enjoy your achievements as well
as your plans . . .

Be yourself. Especially, do not feign affection. Neither
be cynical about love; for in the face of all aridity and
disenchantment it is as perennial as the grass.

Take kindly the counsel of the years, gracefully
surrendering the things of youth. Nurture strength of
spirit to shield you in sudden misfortune. But do not
distress yourself with imaginings. Many fears are born
of fatigue and loneliness. Beyond a wholesome discipline,
be gentle with yourself . . .

Be at peace with God, whatever you conceive Him to be,
and whatever your labours and aspirations, in the noisy *
confusion of life keep peace with your soul.

With all its sham, drudgery and broken dreams, it is
still a beautiful world. Be cheerful. Strive to be happy.

MAX EHRMANN

You were born together, and together you shall be for evermore,
Aye, you shall be together even in the silent memory of God,
But let there be spaces in your togetherness,
and let the winds of heaven dance between you.
Love one another, but make not a bond of love;
Let it rather be a moving sea between the shores of your souls.

Fill each other's cup but drink not from one cup,
Give one another of your bread, but eat not from the same loaf,
Sing and dance together and be joyous, but let each one of you be alone,
Even as the strings of a lute are alone though they quiver with the same music.
Give your hearts, but not into each other's keeping,
For only the hand of life can control your hearts;
And stand together, yet not too near together,
For the pillars of the temple stand apart
And the oak tree and the cypress grow not in each other's shadow.

KAHLIL GIBRAN

When love beckons to you, follow him,
Though his ways are hard and steep.
And when his wings enfold you yield to him,
Though the sword hidden among his pinions may wound you.
And when he speaks to you believe in him,
Though his voice may shatter your dreams as the north wind lays
waste the garden.
For even as love crowns you so shall he crucify you.
Even as he is for your growth so is he for your pruning.
Even as he ascends to your height and caresses your tenderest branches that
quiver in the sun,
So shall he descend to your roots and shake them in their clinging to the earth.
Like sheaves of corn he gathers you unto himself.
He threshes you to make you naked.
He shifts you to free you from your husks.
He grinds you to whiteness.
He kneads you until you are pliant;
And then he assigns you to his sacred fire, that you may become sacred bread
for God's sacred feast.
All these things shall love do unto you that you may know the secrets of your
heart, and in that knowledge become a fragment of Life's heart.
But if in your fear you would seek only love's peace and love's pleasure,
Then it is better for you that you cover your nakedness and pass out of love's
threshing-floor,
Into the seasonless world where you shall laugh, but not all of your laughter,
and weep, but not all of your tears.
Love gives naught but itself and takes naught but from itself.
Love possesses not nor would it be possessed;
For love is sufficient unto love.
When you love you should not say, 'God is in my heart', but rather, 'I am in the
heart of God.'
And think not you can direct the course of love, for love, if it finds you worthy,
directs your course.
Love has no other desire but to fulfil itself.

But if you love and must needs have desires, let these be your desires:
To melt and be like a running brook that sings its melody to the night.
To know the pain of too much tenderness.
To be wounded by your own understanding of love;
And to bleed willingly and joyfully.
To wake at dawn with a winged heart and give thanks for another day of loving;
To rest at the noon hour and meditate love's ecstasy;
To return home at eventide with gratitude;
And then to sleep with a prayer for the beloved in your heart and a song of praise upon your lips.

KAHLIL GIBRAN

The chuppah stands on four poles.
The home has four corners.
The chuppah stands on four poles.
The marriage stands on four legs.
Four points loose the winds
that blow on the walls of the house,
the south wind that brings the warm rain,
the east wind that brings the cold rain,
the north wind that brings the cold sun
and the snow, the long west wind
bringing the weather off the far plains.

Here we live open to the seasons.
Here the winds caress and cuff us
contrary and fierce as bears.
Here the winds are caught and snarling
in the pines, a cat in a net clawing
breaking twigs to fight loose.
Here the winds brush your face
soft in the morning as feathers
that float down from the dove's breast.

Here the moon sails up out of the ocean
dripping like a just washed apple.
Here the sun wakes us like a baby.
Therefore the chuppah has no sides.

It is not a box.
It is not a coffin.
It is not a dead end.
Therefore the chuppah has no walls
We have made a home together
open to the weather of our time.
We are mills that turn in the winds of struggle
converting fierce energy into bread.

The canopy is the cloth of our table
where we share fruit and vegetables
of our labor, where our care for the earth
comes back and we take its body in ours.

The canopy is the cover of our bed
where our bodies open their portals wide,
where we eat and drink the blood
of our love, where the sun shines red
as a swallowed sunrise and we burn
in one furnace of joy molten as steel
and the dream is fresh and flower.

O my love O my love we dance
under the chuppah standing over us
like an animal on its four legs,
like a table on which we set our love
as a feast, like a tent
under which we work
not safe but no longer solitary
in the searing heat of our time.

MARGE PIERCY

Chapter Four

YOU AND ME, LOVE

Come live in my heart,
and pay no rent.

SAMUEL LOVER

Chapter Four

A friend, Celia, had finally met Paul, the man of her dreams. They spent one glorious year together — six months of that married — before Celia died. Beautifully and lovingly cared for by Paul, Celia lived long past the time expected by doctors.

Everyone who attended their wedding was changed by the experience of seeing this special couple make their final commitment, knowing how little time they would have together. Yet it wasn't a sad day. One of the great bonds they shared was humour, and the day was filled with laughter and happiness. To them, marrying was a celebration of life, and so it was a rich and joyous occasion. To me, as their co-celebrant, it was an affirmation of the great healing power of love. Celia and Paul wrote of their relationship 'We found by giving ourselves up, by devoting ourselves to each other, we did not lose, but rather found ourselves.'

The poems in this chapter are very personal declarations of love and commitment. They can be read by the couple who is marrying, but are just as effective read by others.

Our love is like a lovely bridge
Between your heart and mine
A bridge we've built down through the years
Just to our own design.

It's based on happy memories
Of the good times that we've known
The hopes and dreams we two have shared
The thoughtfulness you've shown.

It's stronger now than ever
For it's grown with every smile
And every act of kindness
That makes life seem more worthwhile.

And now I know that, if you're near
Or if we're miles apart
Our love still unites us
With a bridge from heart to heart.

AUTHOR UNKNOWN

MY LOVE SURROUNDS THE HOUSE IN WHICH YOU DWELL

My love surrounds the house in which you dwell,
The place you work, the streets your feet have known,
With more of tenderness than I can tell
And prayers that I have said for you alone.
If you are lonely, know that I am near;
If you are sad, my faith will comfort you.
The things you value I shall hold most dear,
Your happiness will make me happy too.
And be sure of this — though you may travel far,
My love will guide you anywhere you are.

AUTHOR UNKNOWN

VARIATION ON THE WORD 'SLEEP'

I would like to watch you sleeping,
which may not happen.
I would like to watch you,
sleeping. I would like to sleep
with you, to enter
your sleep as its smooth dark wave
slides over my head

and walk with you through that lucent
wavering forest of bluegreen leaves
with its watery sun & three moons
towards the cave where you must descend,
towards your worst fear

I would like to give you the silver
branch, the small white flower, the one
word that will protect you
from the grief at the centre
of your dream, from the grief
at the centre. I would like to follow
you up the long stairway
again & become
the boat that would row you back
carefully, a flame
in two cupped hands
to where your body lies
beside me, and you enter
it as easily as breathing in

I would like to be the air
that inhabits you for a moment
only. I would like to be that unnoticed
& that necessary.

MARGARET ATWOOD

from IN YOUR PRESENCE
(A SONG CYCLE)

In love, what do we love
But to give and to receive
That love by which we live.

You, loved and known and unknown,
Are the one and only one
World I am chosen to dwell in.

I turn in your day and your night
Pivoting on one thought,
What we are and are not,

That love as evergreen mover
Is our always and our never,
Creator, destroyer, preserver.

In the true-knot of your arms
Lock me from the world's alarms;
    To that narrow room
    All kingdoms come.

Waking, dreaming, we shall rove
The warm lands and seas of love,
    And fear no winter there
    Nor anguish on the air,

While feather winds wave us on
Through time coming and time gone,
    Present to us now
    In the sealing of a vow.

CHARLES BRASCH

The tides shall cease to beat the shore,
The stars fall from the sky;
Yet I will love thee more and more
Until the day I die, my dear,
Until the day I die.

ROBERT BURNS

I PROMISE

I promise to give you the best of myself
and to ask of you no more than you can give.

I promise to respect you as your own person
and to realise that your interests, desires and needs
are no less important than my own.

I promise to share with you my time and my attention
and to bring joy, strength and imagination to our relationship.

I promise to keep myself open to you,
to let you see through the window of my world
    into my innermost fears and feelings, secrets and dreams.

I promise to grow along with you,
to be willing to face changes in order to keep
    our relationship alive and exciting.

I promise to love you in good times and in bad,
with all I have to give and all I feel inside in the only way I know how.
Completely and forever.

DOROTHY R. COLGAN

VALENTINE

My heart has made its mind up
And I'm afraid it's you.
Whatever you've got lined up,
My heart has made its mind up
And if you can't be signed up
This year, next year will do.
My heart has made its mind up
And I'm afraid it's you.

WENDY COPE

Not a red rose or a satin heart.

I give you an onion.
It is a moon wrapped in brown paper.
It promises light
like the careful undressing of love.

Here.
It will blind you with tears
like a lover.
It will make your reflection
a wobbling photo of grief.

I am trying to be truthful.

Not a cute card or a kissogram.

I give you an onion.
Its fierce kiss will stay on your lips,
possessive and faithful
as we are,
for as long as we are.

Take it.
Its platinum loops shrink to a wedding-ring,
if you like.

Lethal.
Its scent will cling to your fingers,
cling to your knife.

CAROL ANN DUFFY

To whom I owe the leaping delight
That quickens my senses in our wakingtime
And the rhythm that governs the repose of our sleepingtime,
  The breathing in unison

Of lovers whose bodies smell of each other
Who think the same thoughts without the need of speech
And babble the same speech without need of meaning.

No peevish winter wind shall chill
No sullen tropic sun shall wither
The roses in the rose-garden which is ours and ours only

But this dedication is for others to read:
These are private words addressed to you in public.

T.S. ELIOT

As a room you know,
And even at midnight
Walk through effortlessly,
By sense, not sight
Passing unscathed between
Table and chair
Avoiding the low foot-stool,
Faultlessly aware
Of ledge and bowl
Of flower and crystal vase;
Moving unerringly
Without fear or pause
To the desk with its open book,
Paper-knife, and book-mark:
As this room I would have you know me,
Even in the dark.

RUTH GILBERT

Find me the rose that will not die,
The tree no axe can fell,
The spring no Summer's drought shall dry,
And this last miracle:
Show me the wood, the timeless wood
Where tall and steadfast stands
(The lightning quenched, the storms withstood)
A house not made with hands.

Here is your rose that will not die,
Your tree no axe can fell,
The spring no Summer's drought shall dry,
And here your miracle:
Behold the wood, the timeless wood,
And see how, steadfast, stands
(All lightnings quenched, all storms withstood)
Love's house, not made with hands.

RUTH GILBERT

ABOUT OURSELVES

In our separate lives
We unite
Not merely at meal-times
Or in bed in the illumined night.

Love lives on love and thrives
As it must indeed
On difference. Indifference
is the prerogative of the dead.

Let's look to the now, looking
Trustingly ahead.
For we are two, yet one,
The moon being complementary
To the sun.

Which precedence has moon, has sun?
The heavens' mystery
Is not for mortal woman or for man.

We only know what we have always known,
That without love we live alone.

DENIS GLOVER

This day we shall remember well
As in our married love we dwell
And cast our minds back to this time
You made me yours and I you mine.

In wedded love we choose to be
Each binding each and yet each free
As days and months and years go on
Our love will hold us firm and strong.

The marriage vow this day we say
A vow we'll build on day by day
And as we walk the path of life
The world will know we're man and wife

We two who now are but one soul
Have each to play a different role
And yet we know that all shall see
That bond of love 'twixt you and me.

For in this life we each shall care
That all we do is all times fair
We pledge this day to be as one
In all those wondrous years to come.

BRIAN ZOUCH

Without you every morning would be like going back to work
after a holiday,
Without you I couldn't stand the smell of East Lancs Road,
Without you ghost ferries would cross the Mersey manned by
skeleton crews,
Without you I'd probably feel happy and have more money
and time and nothing to do with it;
Without you I'd have to leave my stillborn poems on other
people's doorsteps, wrapped in brown paper,
Without you there'd never be sauce to put on sausage butties,
Without you plastic flowers in shop windows would just be
plastic flowers in shop windows,
Without you I'd spend my summers picking morosely over
the remains of train crashes,
Without you white birds would wrench themselves free from
my paintings and fly off dripping blood into the night,
Without you green apples wouldn't taste greener,
Without you Mothers wouldn't let their children play out after
tea,
Without you every musician in the world would forget how to
play the blues,
Without you Public Houses would be public again,
Without you the Sunday Times colour supplement would
come out in black-and-white,
Without you indifferent colonels would shrug their shoulders
and press the button,
Without you they'd stop changing the flowers in Piccadilly
Gardens,
Without you Clark Kent would forget how to become
Superman,
Without you Sunshine Breakfast would only consist of
Cornflakes,
Without you there'd be no colour in Magic colouring books,

Without you Mahler's 8th would only be performed by street
   musicians in derelict houses,
Without you they'd forget to put the salt in every packet of
   crisps,
Without you it would be an offence punishable by a fine of up
   to £200 or two months' imprisonment to be found in
   possession of curry powder,
Without you riot police are massing in quiet sidestreets,
Without you all streets would be one-way the other way,
Without you there'd be no one not to kiss goodnight when we
   quarrel,
Without you the first martian to land would turn round and go
   away again,
Without you they'd forget to change the weather,
Without you blind men would sell unlucky heather,
Without you there would be
no landscapes/no stations/no houses,
no chipshops/no quiet villages/no seagulls
on beaches/no hopscotch on pavements/no night/no
   morning/there'd be no city no country,
Without you.

ADRIAN HENRI

SCAFFOLDING

Masons, when they start upon a building,
Are careful to test out the scaffolding;

Make sure that planks won't slip at busy points,
Secure all ladders, tighten bolted joints.

And yet all this comes down when the job's done
Showing off walls of sure and solid stone.

So if, my dear, there sometimes seem to be
Old bridges breaking between you and me

Never fear. We may let the scaffolds fall
Confident that we have built our wall.

SEAMUS HEANEY

from WINESONG 15

I will sing a lovesong
— do not hide your ears
it is time for heartsongs and it is time for tears —
lady, I am a lover
lady, I am a thief
and I need your heart, love
as I need wine and tide and beach

KERI HULME

INVENTING YOU

If I were to forget
the way I think of you
break you to bits
jumble you up
and sweep away all sign of you
and then if I were to start
all over again
and invent you
with nothing more to work on
than a notion
of your waiting to be discovered
I would not approach the problem
by trying to make you solid
giving you shape
attaching so many yards
of pretended skin
to so much meat and bone

the museums are full
of lively examples
of that kind of solution
but when the attendants
are not looking
my touch detects stone

instead
I would take silence
and begin with one sound
then another
to fill first the air
and the seas and the forests

then the towns
with your softness
if I were to forget
the way I think of you
and then invent you
all over again
I would assemble you
from sigh and laughter
from half-words and half-cries
from heartbeat
the click of bone

breathing in and breathing out
from all sound of true love
even the rub the skin makes
touching in sleep

KEVIN IRELAND

EPIC FILM

from SUMMER WITH MONIKA

Our love will be an epic film
With dancing songs and laughter
The kind in which the lovers meet
And live happy ever after
Our love will be a famous play
With lots of bedroom scenes
You are twenty-two you are monika
And only we know what that means

ROGER MCGOUGH

TAKING THE TIME

Taking time to love
is what it's all about —
what makes the clocks turn
and the sunsets come
true and without
          complication.

That doesn't mean
lying close
  in shut-up rooms
or staying always
          face to face.

It's meant to cover walking,
being apart and knowing
that coming back together
makes small distances
          even smaller.

And taking the time to love
is, most of all, caring enough
to not hold on too tightly
and yet not run too loose.

ROD MCKUEN

THE CONFIRMATION

Yes, yours, my love, is the right human face.
I in my mind had waited for this long,
Seeing the false and searching for the true,
Then found you as a traveller finds a place
Of welcome suddenly amid the wrong
Valleys and rocks and twisting roads. But you,
What shall I call you? A fountain in a waste,
A well of water in a country dry,
Or anything that's honest and good, an eye
That makes the whole world bright. Your open heart,
Simple with giving, gives the primal deed,
The first good world, the blossom, the blowing seed,
The hearth, the steadfast land, the wandering sea,
Not beautiful or rare in every part,
But like yourself, as they were meant to be.

EDWIN MUIR

Today I will marry my best friend.
The one I have laughed and cried with,
The one I have learned from and shared with,
The one I have chosen to support, encourage
And give myself to through all these days
God has given us to share.

HUGH PRATHER

A POEM OF BLISS

We are placed on a wedding cake
like two dolls, bride and groom.
When the knife strikes
we'll try to stay on the same slice.

RONNY SOMECK, TRANSLATED BY YAIR MAZOR

When I was lonely
Your fingers reached for mine, their touch
Natural as sunlight's.

When I was hardened
Your warmness thawed my rock as gently
As music thought.

When I was angry
You smiled: 'But this day is short
For these long shadows.'

When I was solemn
You held out laughter, casual as light
For a cigarette.

When I was troubled
Your understanding crossed the bounds of
Words to silence.

When I was frightened
Your eyes said: 'Fear's a child's dream. I too
Have dreamed and woken.'

A.S.J. TESSIMOND

LIKE LAMPLIGHT

One day when you are beside me
invite me to speak
of the secrets I never knew
I wanted to tell you, of the warmth
I never knew I owned
until you released it
by moving close as lamplight seems
to glass. Ask me

why I came to you
with the reverence of one
who sees a flower bloom
where none has bloomed before.
By saying what it is
I will have said what was.

Sometimes when you are content
ask me what it is
that moves me to want to hold you so,
so often, and laugh when I tell
you the same old
indestructible thing.

One day when you are
where you need no invitation to be
I will tell you
how you flower
like lamplight in me.

BRIAN TURNER

ALL THE WHILE

Upstairs to my downstairs
echo to my silence
you walk through my veins shopping
and spin food from my sleep

I hear your small noises
you hide in closets without handles
you surprise me from the cellar
your foot-soles bright black

You slip in and out of beauty
And imply that nothing is wrong
Who sent you?
What is your assignment?

Though years sneak by like children
You stay as unaccountable
as the underwear set to soak
in the bowl where I brush my teeth

JOHN UPDIKE

From SONG OF THE OPEN ROAD

1

Afoot and light-hearted I take to the open road,
Healthy, free, the world before me,
The long brown path before me leading wherever I choose.

11

Listen! I will be honest with you,
I do not offer the old smooth prizes, but offer rough new prizes,
These are the days that must happen to you:
You shall not heap up what is call'd riches,
You shall scatter with lavish hand all that you earn or achieve . . .

15

Camerado, I give you my hand!
I give you my love more precious than money,
I give you myself before preaching or law;
Will you give me yourself? Will you come travel with me?
Shall we stick by each other as long as we live?

WALT WHITMAN

Chapter Five

LAUGHTER AND LOVE

By all means marry; if you get a
good wife, you'll be happy. If
you get a bad one, you'll become
a philosopher.

SOCRATES

Among those whom I like or
admire, I can find no common
denominator, but among those
whom I love, I can: all of them
make me laugh.

W.H. AUDEN

Chapter Five

Humour is a great common ground, a salve to hurt feelings, and a potent aphrodisiac. Again and again, couples tell me, 'He really makes me laugh' or 'We laugh together all the time'. One couple's greatest bonding moment happened early on in their relationship when she laughed so much at something he said that she snorted soft drink out of her nose and into his eye.

Because in my other life I am a comedian, I am often asked if weddings are a comedy routine for me. Of course, they're not. However, one of the delightful aspects of being a celebrant for me is that I can bring my own personality to it, although like most comedians, I'm not a constant crack-up. My most important goal is to create a ceremony that the couple want, that reflects them and their relationship.

Some couples want a ceremony that is very formal, or very deep and romantic. Others want something much more relaxed, and that sometimes includes a laugh. 'The Owl and the Pussy-Cat' is very popular, and the greatest laugh usually occurs for the line 'So they took it away, and were married next day/By the Turkey who lives on the hill', when all eyes turn to see my reaction!

Often humour in a ceremony is unintentional. One very nervous English couple, marrying while holidaying in Wellington, had a very small wedding, which was being video-taped for loved ones at home. The groom held his bride's hand and repeated his vows solemnly after me:
'Jane, I promise to love you eternally . . .'
'Jane, I promise,' he stumbled, 'to love you internally . . .'
No one laughed harder than the couple themselves.

Like any family gathering, a well-planned surprise at a wedding can be delightful. One groom, on promising to endow his bride with all his worldly goods, produced, not the ring, but an American Express gold card.

4lb of love
$^1/_2$lb of good looks
1lb of sweet temper
1lb of butter of youth
1lb of blindness to faults
1lb of pounded wit
1lb of good humour
2 tablespoons of sweet argument
1 pint of rippling laughter
1 wine glass of common sense
dash of modesty.

Put the love, good looks and sweet temper into a well-furnished house.
Beat the butter of youth to a cream, and mix well together with the blindness
to faults. Stir the pounded wit and good humour into the sweet argument,
then add the rippling laughter and common sense. Add a dash of modesty and
work the whole together until everything is well mixed.
Bake gently forever.

AUTHOR UNKNOWN

Have dinner ready. Plan ahead, even the night before, to have a delicious meal ready in time for his return. This is a way of letting him know that you have been thinking about him, and are concerned about his needs. Most men are hungry when they come home, and the prospect of a good meal (especially his favourite dish) is part of the warm welcome needed.

Prepare yourself: take 15 minutes to rest so you'll be refreshed when he arrives. Touch up your make-up, put a ribbon in your hair and be fresh-looking. He has just been with a lot of work-weary people.

Be a little gay and a little more interesting for him. His boring day may need a lift, and one of your duties is to provide it.

Clear away the clutter. Make one last trip through the main part of the house just before your husband arrives.

Gather up schoolbooks, toys, paper etc, and then run a dust cloth over the tables.

Over the cooler months of the year you should prepare and light a fire for him to unwind by. Your husband will feel he has reached a haven of rest and order, and it will give you a lift, too. After all, catering for his comfort will provide you with immense personal satisfaction.

Prepare the children, take a few minutes to wash their hands and faces (if they are small), comb their hair, and if necessary, change their clothes. They are little treasures and he would like to see them playing the part.

Minimise all noise. At the time of his arrival, eliminate all noise from the washer, dryer, and vacuum. Try to encourage the children to be quiet.

Be happy to see him. Greet him with a warm smile and show sincerity in your desire to please him.

Listen to him. You may have a dozen important things to tell him, but the moment of his arrival is not the time. Let him talk first. Remember, his topics of conversation are more important than yours.

Make the evening his. Never complain if he comes home late or goes out to dinner or other places of entertainment without you; instead, try to understand his world of strain and pressure, and his very real need to be at home and relax.

Your goal is to try to make sure your home is a place of peace, order and tranquility where your husband can renew himself in body and spirit.

Don't greet him with complaints and problems.

Don't complain if he's late for dinner, or even if he stays out all night. Count this as minor compared to what he might have gone through that day.

Make him comfortable. Have him lean back in a comfortable chair or have him lie down in the bedroom. Have a cool or warm drink ready for him.

Arrange his pillow and offer to take off his shoes. Speak in a low, soothing and pleasant voice.

Don't ask him questions about his actions, or question his judgement or integrity. Remember, he is the master of the house, and as such will always exercise his will with fairness and truthfulness. You have no right to question him.

A good wife always knows her place.

AN EXTRACT FROM *HOUSEKEEPING MONTHLY*, 13 MAY 1955

The soldier loves his rifle,
    The scholar loves his books,
The farmer loves his horses,
    The filmstar loves her looks.
There's love the whole world over
    Wherever you may be;
Some lose their rest for gay Mae West,
    But you're my cup of tea.

Some talk of Alexander
    And some of Fred Astaire,
Some like their heroes hairy
    Some like them debonair,
Some prefer a curate
    And some an ADC,
Some like a tough to treat 'em rough,
    But you're my cup of tea.

Some are mad on Airedales
    And some on Pekinese,
On tabby cats or parrots
    Or guinea pigs or geese.
There are patients in asylums
    Who think that they're a tree;
I had an aunt who loved a plant,
    But you're my cup of tea.

Some have sagging waistlines
    And some a bulbous nose
And some a floating kidney
    And some have hammer toes
Some have tennis elbow
    And some have housemaid's knee,
And some I know have got BO,
    But you're my cup of tea.

The blackbird loves the earthworm,
    The adder loves the sun,
The polar bear an iceberg,
    The elephant a bun,
The trout enjoys the river,
    The whale enjoys the sea,
And dogs love most an old lamp-post,
    But you're my cup of tea.

W. H. AUDEN

Some say that love's a little boy,
    And some say he's a bird,
Some say he makes the world go round,
    And some say that's absurd:
And when I asked the man next door
    Who looked as if he knew,
His wife was very cross indeed,
    And said it wouldn't do.

Does it look like a pair of pyjamas
    Or the ham in a temperance hotel,
Does its odour remind one of llamas
    Or has it a comforting smell?
Is it prickly to touch as a hedge is
    Or soft as eiderdown fluff,
Is it sharp or quite smooth at the edges?
    O tell me the truth about love.

The history books refer to it
    In cryptic little notes,
And it's a common topic on
    The TransAtlantic boats;
I've found the subject mentioned in
    Accounts of suicides,
And even seen it scribbled on
    The backs of railway guides.

Does it howl like a hungry Alsatian
    Or boom like a military band,
Could one give a first-class imitation
    On a saw or a Steinway Grand,
Is its singing at parties a riot,
    Does it only like Classical stuff,
Will it stop when one wants to be quiet?
    O tell me the truth about love.

I looked inside the summer-house,
    It wasn't ever there,
I tried the Thames at Maidenhead
    And Brighton's bracing air;
I don't know what the blackbird sang
    Or what the roses said;
But it wasn't in the chicken-run
    Or underneath the bed.

Can it pull extraordinary faces,
    Is it usually sick on a swing,
Does it spend all its time at the races
    Or fiddling with pieces of string,
Has it views of its own about money,
    Does it think Patriotism enough,
Are its stories vulgar but funny?
    O tell me the truth about love . . .

When it comes, will it come without warning
    Just as I'm picking my nose,
Will it knock on my door in the morning
    Or tread in the bus on my toes,
Will it come like a change in the weather,
    Will its greeting be courteous or bluff,
Will it alter my life altogether?
    O tell me the truth about love.

W. H. AUDEN

Yes, I'll marry you, my dear,
And here's the reason why;
So I can push you out of bed
When the baby starts to cry,
And if we hear a knocking
And it's creepy and it's late,
Hand you the torch you see,
And you investigate.

Yes, I'll marry you, my dear,
You may not apprehend it,
But when the tumble-drier goes
It's you that has to mend it,
You have to face the neighbour
Should our Labrador attack him,
And if a drunkard fondles me
It's you that has to whack him.

Yes, I'll marry you,
You're virile and you're lean,
My house is like a pigsty
You can help to keep it clean.
That sexy little dinner
Which you serve by candlelight,
As I do chipolatas,
You can cook it every night!

It's you who has to work the drill
And put up curtain track,
And when I've got PMT it's you who gets the flak,
I do see great advantages,
But none of them for you,
And so before you see the light,
I do, I do, I do!

PAM AYRES

The Owl and the Pussy-Cat went to sea
    In a beautiful pea-green boat.
They took some honey, and plenty of money,
    Wrapped up in a five-pound note.
The Owl looked up to the stars above
    And sang to a small guitar,
'O lovely Pussy! O Pussy, my love,
What a beautiful Pussy you are,
    Your are, you are!
What a beautiful Pussy you are!'

Pussy said to the Owl, 'You elegant fowl!
    How charmingly sweet you sing!
O let us be married! Too long have we tarried:
But what shall we do for a ring?'
They sailed away, for a year and a day,
    To the land where the Bong-Tree grows,
And there in the wood a Piggy-wig stood,
With a ring at the end of his nose,
    His nose, his nose!
With a ring at the end of his nose.

'Dear Pig, are you willing to sell for one shilling
    Your ring?' Said the Piggy, 'I will'.
So they took it away, and were married next day
    By the Turkey who lives on the hill.
They dined on mince, and slices of quince,
    Which they ate with a runcible spoon;
And hand in hand, on the edge of the sand
They danced by the light of the moon,
    The moon, the moon,
They danced by the light of the moon.

EDWARD LEAR

Wherever I am, there's always Pooh,
There's always Pooh and Me.
Whatever I do, he wants to do,
'Where are you going to-day?' says Pooh:
'Well, that's very odd 'cos I was too.
'Let's go together,' says Pooh, says he.
'Let's go together,' says Pooh.

'What's twice eleven?' I said to Pooh,
('Twice what?' said Pooh to Me.)
'I *think* it ought to be twenty-two.'
'Just what I think myself,' said Pooh.
'It wasn't an easy sum to do,
But that's what it is,' said Pooh, said he.
'That's what it is,' said Pooh.

'Let's look for dragons,' I said to Pooh.
'Yes, let's,' said Pooh to Me.
We crossed the river and found a few —
'Yes, those are dragons all right,' said Pooh.
'As soon as I saw their beaks I knew.
That's what they are,' said Pooh, said he.
'That's what they are,' said Pooh.

'Let's frighten the dragons,' I said to Pooh.
'That's right,' said Pooh to Me.
'*I'm* not afraid,' I said to Pooh,
And I held his paw and I shouted 'Shoo!
Silly old dragons!' – and off they flew.
'I wasn't afraid,' said Pooh, said he,
'I'm *never* afraid with you.'

So wherever I am, there's always Pooh,
There's always Pooh and Me.
'What would I do,' I said to Pooh,
'If it wasn't for you,' and Pooh said: 'True,
It isn't much fun for One, but Two
Can stick together,' says Pooh, says he.
'That's how it is,' says Pooh.

A.A. MILNE (1882-1956)

ten milk bottles standing in the hall
ten milk bottles up against the wall
next door neighbour thinks we're dead
hasn't heard a sound he said
doesn't know we've been in bed
the ten whole days since we were wed

noone knows and noone sees
we lovers doing what we please
but people stop and point at these
ten milk bottles a-turning into cheese

ten milk bottles standing day and night
ten different thicknesses and
different shades of white
persistent carolsingers without a note to utter
silent carolsingers a-turning into butter

now she's run out of passion
and there's not much left in me
so maybe we'll get up
and make a cup of tea
then people can stop wondering
what they're waiting for
those ten milk bottles a-queuing at our door
those ten milk bottles a-queuing at our door

ROGER MCGOUGH

A WORD TO HUSBANDS

To keep your marriage brimming,
With love in the loving cup,
Whenever you're wrong, admit it;
Whenever you're right, shut up.

OGDEN NASH

How wise I am to have instructed the butler to instruct the first footman to
    instruct the second footman to instruct
    the doorman to order my carriage;
I am about to volunteer a definition of marriage.
Just as I know there are two Hagens, Walter and Copen,
I know that marriage is a legal and religious alliance entered into by a man who
    can't sleep with the window shut,
    and a woman who can't sleep with the window open.
Moreover, just as I am unsure of the difference between
flora and fauna, and flotsam and jetsam,
I am quite sure that marriage is the alliance of two people one of whom never
    remembers birthdays, and the other never forgetsam,
And he refuses to believe there is a leak in the water pipe or the gas pipe and
    she is convinced she is about to asphyxiate or drown.
And she says Quick get up and get my hairbrushes off the windowsill,
    it's raining in, and he replies Oh they're all right, it's only raining straight
    down.
That is why marriage is so much more interesting than divorce,
Because it's the only known example of the happy meeting of the immovable
    object with the irresistible force.
So I hope husbands and wives will continue to debate and combat over
    everything debatable and combatable,
Because I believe a little incompatibility is the spice of life,
    particularly if he has income and she is pattable.

OGDEN NASH

WHAT ALMOST EVERY WOMAN KNOWS
SOONER OR LATER

Husbands are things that wives have to get used to putting up with,
And with whom they breakfast with and sup with.
They interfere with the discipline of nurseries,
And forget anniversaries,
And when they have been particularly remiss
They think they can cure everything with a great big kiss,
And when you tell them about something awful they have done they just
    look unbearably patient and smile a superior smile,
And think, Oh she'll get over it after a while.
And they always drink cocktails faster than they can assimilate them,
And if you look in their direction they act as if they were martyrs and
    you were trying to sacrifice, or immolate them,
And when it's a question of walking five miles to play golf they are very
    energetic but if it's doing anything useful around the house they are
    very lethargic,
And then they tell you that women are unreasonable and don't know
    anything about logic,
And they never want to get up or go to bed at the same time as you do,
And when you perform some simple common or garden rite like putting
    cold cream on your face or applying a touch of lipstick they seem to
    think you are up to some kind of black magic like a priestess of Voodoo.
And they are brave and calm and cool and collected about the ailments
    of the person they have promised to honor and cherish,
But the minute they get a sniffle or a stomachache of their own, why
    you'd think they were about to perish,
And when you are alone with them they ignore all the minor courtesies
    and as for airs and graces, they utterly lack them,
But when there are a lot of people around they hand you so many chairs
    and ashtrays and sandwiches and butter you with such bowings and
    scrapings that you want to smack them.
Husbands are indeed an irritating form of life,
And yet through some quirk of Providence most of them are really very
    deeply ensconced in the affection of their wife.

OGDEN NASH

Though you know it anyhow
Listen to me, darling, now,

Proving what I need not prove
How I know I love you, love.

Near and far, near and far,
I am happy where you are;

Likewise I have never larnt
How to be it where you aren't.

Far and wide, far and wide,
I can walk with you beside;

Furthermore, I tell you what,
I sit and sulk where you are not.

Visitors remark my frown
Where you're upstairs and I am down,

Yes, and I'm afraid I pout
When I'm indoors and you are out;

But how contentedly I view
Any room containing you.

In fact I care not where you be,
Just as long as it's with me.

In all your absences I glimpse
Fire and flood and trolls and imps.

Is your train a minute slothful?
I goad the stationmaster wrothful.

When with friends to bridge you drive
I never know if you're alive,

And when you linger late in shops
I long to telephone the cops.

Yet how worth the waiting for,
To see you coming through the door.

Somehow, I can be complacent
Never but with you adjacent.

Near and far, near and far,
I am happy where you are;

Likewise I have never larnt
How to be it where you aren't.

Then grudge me not my fond endeavor,
To hold you in my sight forever;

Let none, not even you, disparage
Such a valid reason for a marriage.

OGDEN NASH

A single flow'r he sent me, since we met.
    All tenderly his messenger he chose;
Deep-hearted, pure, with scented dew still wet —
    One perfect rose.

I knew the language of the floweret;
    'My fragile leaves,' it said, 'his heart enclose.'
Love long has taken for his amulet
    One perfect rose.

Why is it no one ever sent me yet
    One perfect limousine, do you suppose?
Ah no, it's always just my luck to get
    One perfect rose.

DOROTHY PARKER

MR EDWARDS
Myfanwy Price!

MISS PRICE
Mr Mog Edwards!

MR EDWARDS
I am a draper mad with love. I love you more than all the flannelette and calico, candlewick, dimity, crash and merino, tussore, cretonne, crepon, muslin, poplin, ticking and twill in the whole Cloth Hall of the world. I have come to take you away to my Emporium on the hill, where the change hums on wires. Throw away your little bedsocks and your Welsh wool knitted jacket, I will warm the sheets like an electric toaster, I will lie by your side like the Sunday roast . . .

MISS PRICE
I will knit you a wallet of forget-me-not blue, for the money to be comfy. I will warm your heart by the fire so that you can slip it in under your vest when the shop is closed . . .

MR EDWARDS
Myfanwy, Myfanwy, before the mice gnaw at your bottom drawer will you say

MISS PRICE
Yes, Mog, yes, Mog, yes, yes, yes . . .

MR EDWARDS
And all the bells of the tills of the town shall ring for our wedding.

DYLAN THOMAS

Chapter Six

PROSE LOVE

It is a truth universally
acknowledged, that a man in
possession of a large fortune
must be in want of a wife.

JANE AUSTEN
PRIDE AND PREJUDICE

Chapter Six

PROSE LOVE

Prose readings can encompass all sorts of favourite words. Excerpts from novels, children's books, plays, film scripts, and even song lyrics can be read aloud at weddings and commitment ceremonies.

Reading the works that make up this book, I am always reminded of the timelessness and universality of love. The joy Elizabeth Barrett felt on receiving a letter from Robert Browning was just as intense as one bride-to-be who showed me the little cache of saved text messages from her sweetheart. Perhaps Robert Browning's letters were more eloquent than 'Lv u babe', but for both recipients, the feeling was the same.

One groom told me of his loneliness when he was a single man. Shortly after meeting his beloved, he made a planned trip overseas without her. Despite her absence, the warmth of her love travelled with him. 'Even though she wasn't there, that sense of loneliness was gone.' His words echo those of Victor Hugo in *Les Misèrables:* 'Love is knowing that even when you are alone, you will never be lonely again.'

Love is friendship that has caught fire. It's quiet understanding, mutual confidence, sharing and forgiving. It's loyalty through good times and bad. It settles for less than perfection, and makes allowances for human weakness.

Love is content with the present, hopes for the future, and refuses to brood over the past. It's the day-in and day-out chronicle of irritations, problems, compromises, small disappointments, big victories, and working together towards common goals.

If you have love in your life, it can make up for a great many things that you lack. If you don't, no matter what else there is — it's not enough.

ANN LANDERS

Love is a temporary madness, it erupts like volcanoes and then subsides. And when it subsides you have to make a decision. You have to work out whether your roots have so entwined together that it is inconceivable that you should ever part.

Because this is what love is. Love is not breathlessness, it is not excitement, it is not the promulgation of eternal passion. That is just being 'in love', which any fool can do.

Love itself is what is left over when being in love has burned away, and this is both an art and a fortunate accident. Those that truly love, have roots that grow towards each other underground, and when all the pretty blossoms have fallen from their branches, they find that they are one tree, and not two.

LOUIS DE BERNIÈRES

It is a short word, but it contains all: it means the body, the soul, the life, the entire being. We feel it as we feel the warmth of the blood, we breathe it as we breathe the air, we carry it in ourselves as we carry our thoughts. Nothing more exists for us. It is not a word; it is an inexpressible state indicated by four letters.

GUY DE MAUPASSANT

Love does not consist in gazing at each other, but in looking outward together in the same direction.

For in fact, man and woman are not only looking outward in the same direction, they are working outward. Here one forms ties, roots, a firm base.

Here one makes oneself part of the community of men, of human society. Here the bonds of marriage are formed.

For marriage, which is always spoken of as a bond, becomes, actually, in this stage, many bonds, many strands, of different texture and strength, making up a web that is taut and firm. The web is fashioned of love.

Yes, but many kinds of love: romantic love first, then a slow-growing devotion and, playing through these, a constantly rippling companionship.

It is made of loyalties, and interdependencies, and shared experiences. It is woven of memories; of meetings and conflicts; of triumphs and disappointments.

It is a web of communication, a common language, and the acceptance of lack of language too, a knowledge of likes and dislikes, of habits and reactions, both physical and mental. It is a web of instincts and intuitions, and known and unknown exchanges.

The web of marriage is made by propinquity, in the day-to-day living side by side, looking outward and working outward in the same direction. It is woven in space and in time of the substance of life itself.

ANTOINE DE SAINT-EXUPÉRY

'We are too old to be single. Why shouldn't we both be married, instead of sitting through the long winter evenings by our solitary firesides? Why shouldn't we make one fireside of it . . .

'Let's be a comfortable couple and take care of each other! And if we should get deaf, or lame, or blind, or bed-ridden, how glad we shall be that we have somebody we are fond of, always to talk to and sit with! Let's be a comfortable couple. Now do, my dear!'

CHARLES DICKENS

You can give without loving, but you can never love without giving. The great acts of love are done by those who are habitually performing small acts of kindness. We pardon to the extent that we love. Love is knowing that even when you are alone, you will never be lonely again. And great happiness of life is the conviction that we are loved. Loved for ourselves. And even loved in spite of ourselves.

VICTOR HUGO

We all want to fall in love. Why? Because that experience makes us feel completely alive. Where every sense is heightened, every emotion is magnified, our everyday reality is shattered and we are flying into the heavens. It may only last a moment, an hour, an afternoon. But that doesn't diminish its value. Because we are left with memories that we treasure for the rest of our lives.

RICHARD LA GRAVENESE

I will have poetry in my life. And adventure. And love. Love above all. No . . . not the artful postures of love, not playful and poetical games of love for the amusement of an evening, but love that . . . overthrows life. Unbiddable, ungovernable — like a riot in the heart and nothing to be done, come ruin or rapture. Love — like there has never been in a play.

MARC NORMAN AND TOM STOPPARD

Our life together had been built on mutual choices. We had chosen each other as partners, chosen to love, to trust, and to create joy together. The universe may very well have had a hand in bringing us together; what we did beyond that point was of our own choosing.

That tiny flash of time left me forever changed. I realised that somewhere among the pages of our history, rich in passages of shared memories, we had chosen to become soulmates.

TERRI MCPHERSON

I think the time has come, it really has come for us to do a little courting. Have we ever had time to stand under trees and tell our love? Or to sit down by the sea and make fragrant zones for each other? . . . Do you know the peculiar exquisite scent of a tea-rose? Do you know how the flower bud opens — so unlike other roses and how deep red the thorns are and almost purple the leaves?

. . . Wander with me ten years — will you darling? Ten years in the sun. It's not long — only ten springs.

KATHERINE MANSFIELD

MARRIAGE JOINS TWO PEOPLE IN THE CIRCLE OF ITS LOVE

Marriage joins two people in the circle of its love.

Marriage is a commitment to life, the best that two people can find and bring out in each other. It offers opportunities for sharing and growth that no other relationship can equal. It is a physical and an emotional joining that is promised for a lifetime.

Within the circle of its love, marriage encompasses all of life's most important relationships. A wife and a husband are each other's best friend, confidant, lover, teacher, listener and critic. And there may come times when one partner is heartbroken or ailing, and the love of the other may resemble the tender caring of a parent for a child.

Marriage deepens and enriches every facet of life. Happiness is fuller, memories are fresher, commitment is stronger, even anger is felt more strongly, and passes away more quickly.

Marriage understands and forgives the mistakes life is unable to avoid. It encourages and nurtures new life, new experiences and new ways of expressing a love that is deeper than life.

When two people pledge their love and care for each other in marriage, they create a spirit unique unto themselves which binds them closer than any spoken or written words. Marriage is a promise, a potential made in the hearts of two people who love each other, and takes a lifetime to fulfil.

EDMUND O'NEILL

VIOLET
Ooh, I'm so happy I don't want to go any further. I want to stay right here.
Right on this threshold. To have it lying in front of me, looming on the horizon.
I want the anticipation to last and last. Oh, Jack, I don't want the domestics
and the day-to-day to swallow us. I want us always to recognise each
other's . . . newness. Do you understand? And not to tie each other into
forever because of the ring. But to be with each other because it's marvellous
and not only because we're married.

LORAE PARRY

The most wonderful of all things in life is the discovery of another human being with whom one's relationship has a growing depth, beauty and joy as the years increase. This inner progressiveness of love between two human beings is a most marvellous thing; it cannot be found by looking for it or by passionately wishing for it. It is a sort of divine accident, and the most wonderful of all things in life.

SIR HUGH WALPOLE

'What is REAL?' asked the Rabbit one day, when they were lying side by side near the nursery fender . . . 'Does it mean having things that buzz inside you and a stick-out handle?'

'Real isn't how you're made,' said the Skin Horse. 'It's a thing that happens to you. When a child loves you for a long, long time, not just to play with, but REALLY loves you, then you become Real.'

'Does it hurt?' asked the Rabbit.

'Sometimes,' said the Skin Horse, for he was always truthful. 'When you are Real you don't mind being hurt.'

'Does it happen all at once, like being wound up,' he asked,'or bit by bit?'

'It doesn't happen all at once,' said the Skin Horse.'You become. It takes a long time. That's why it doesn't often happen to people who break easily, or have sharp edges, or who have to be carefully kept. Generally, by the time you are Real, most of your hair has been loved off, and your eyes drop out, and you get loose in the joints and very shabby. But these things don't matter at all, because once you are Real you can't be ugly, except to people who don't understand.'

MARGERY WILLIAMS

Chapter Seven

WISHES FOR LOVE

Love 'em for what they are, and
forgive 'em for what they ain't.

GRANDPA

Chapter Seven

WISHES FOR LOVE

Asking someone to read at a wedding can be a way of including someone who is special to the couple, but not part of the official wedding party. At one small, intimate wedding I attended, the couple's two little daughters took it in turns to read 'The Owl and the Pussy-Cat'. This gave the children something special to do at the service — and in the hectic week before the wedding, the parents were able to say 'Go and practise your reading!'

Parents of the couple often feel neglected at this time, and reading a special poem can make them feel part of the ceremony. In the past, mothers and fathers had definite roles in the wedding — often to the exclusion of the couple themselves.

One mother confided to me that she felt sidelined at first, unsure whether offers to help would be construed as 'interfering'. 'My mother ran my wedding, I just turned up. I don't want my daughter to have that,' she told me. She wrote a beautiful poem for her daughter's wedding, and read it with great feeling.

Today is the day you will always remember
— The greatest in anyone's life
You start off the day just two people in love
And end it as husband and wife.

It's a brand new beginning, the start of a journey
With moments to cherish and treasure
And although there'll be times when you both disagree
These will surely be outweighed by pleasure.

You'll have heard many words of advice in the past
When the secrets of marriage were spoken,
But you know that the answers lie hidden inside
Where the bond of true love lies unbroken.

So live happy for ever — as lovers and friends
It's the dawn of a new life for you
As you stand there together with love in your eyes
From the moment you whisper 'I do'.

And with luck, all your hopes, and your dreams can be real
May success find its way to your hearts
Tomorrow can bring you the greatest of joys
But today is the day it all starts.

AUTHOR UNKNOWN

FRIENDS

There is no better way
To live on this earth
Than to be friends,
Friends who will always
Love and
Stand by each other
'Til life's end.

Friends,
Who will share
Their lives together
Through good times
And bad, and
Who will bring joy
And comfort
To each other
When times are sad.

Friends,
Who will always
Stand together,
And stand strong.
To help share with life's burdens,
To help each other carry on,
Through the tears, through the pain,
Through the sun, through the rain,
No matter what happens to them,
As friends, they will always remain.

And
So it is
That your friendship
Now has grown into love,
And into marriage,
Into a love
That is so beautiful to see.

So may your love
And your friendship
As you begin
Your life together
Last you for an eternity,
And as friends
May you both
Forever be.

AUTHOR UNKNOWN

THE ONE

When the one whose hand you're holding
Is the one who holds your heart,
When the one whose eyes you gaze into
Gives your hopes and dreams their start,
When the one you think of first and last
Is the one who holds you tight,
And the things you plan together
Make the whole world seem just right,
When the one whom you believe in
Puts their faith and trust in you,
You've found the one and only love
You'll share your whole life through.

AUTHOR UNKNOWN

We will not wish you joy on this great day,
For joy is in your hearts and goes with you
Along the fragrant, mystic, sun-lit way:
We will not wish you joy while love is new.

But this is our wish — may you be strong enough
To shelter love, and keep it safe from harm,
When winds blow high, and roads are steep and rough,
May you protect your love, preserve its charm.

When days are dark, may love be your sure light.
When days are cold, may love be your bright fire,
Your guiding star when hope is out of sight,
The essence and sun of your desire.

May love be with you through the flight of years,
Then after the storms, there will always be calm.
Though you have cause for heartache and for tears,
Despair lasts not, where love is there for balm.

This be the prayer we breathe for you today:
When you have reached the summit of life's hill,
May it be possible for you to say,
'Married long years, but we are lovers still.'

AUTHOR UNKNOWN

WE WISH YOU THESE GIFTS

We come today to join in your gladness,
With gifts to show the love we feel for you.
Gifts to grace your home with brightness and with beauty.

But we would also give you gifts of greater value,
That will not age, nor fade, nor wear away.
And so we bring along with earthly blessings
A store of wishes for your wedding day.

May you have memories to share together
A precious treasure gathered through the years
Of happy hours and troubles met and vanquished,
The gold of laughter and the jewels of tears.

We wish you love, deep warm and tender,
More deep and fragrant through each passing day,
Through cloud and sunshine, steadfast and unchanging;
Love that gives and seeks not her own.

We wish you joy in fullest measure,
That every day be filled
With joyful, happy things.

We wish you patience, gentleness and kindness,
Hope that does not wilt nor fade,
Courage, strong and unafraid,
And faith that does not falter.

We wish you sympathy and sense,
Calmness and confidence,
Always with a twinkle in your eyes.

We wish you the peace that passes understanding
To guard your hearts whatever may betide.

AUTHOR UNKNOWN

Carry her over the water,
    And set her down under the tree,
Where the culvers white all day and all night,
    And the winds from every quarter
Sing agreeably, agreeably, agreeably of love.

Put a gold ring on her finger,
    And press her close to your heart,
While the fish in the lake their snapshots take,
    And the frog, that sanguine singer,
Sings agreeably, agreeably, agreeably of love.

The streets shall flock to your marriage,
    The houses turn round to look,
The tables and chairs say suitable prayers,
    And the horses drawing your carriage
Sing agreeably, agreeably, agreeably of love.

W.H. AUDEN

WEDDING SONG

Now you are married
try to love the world
as much as you love
each other. Greet it as your husband,
wife. Love it with all your
might as you sleep
breathing against its back.

Love the world, when, late at night,
you come home to find snails
stuck to the side of the house
like decoration.

Love your neighbours.
The red berries on their trampoline
their green wheelbarrow.

Love the man walking on
water, the man up a
mast. Love the light moving
across the *Island Princess*.

Love your grandmother when she tells you
her hair is three-quarters 'café au lait'.

Try to love the world, even when you discover
there is no such thing as *The Author*
any more.

Love the world, praise
god, even, when your aerobics instructor
is silent.

Try very hard to love
your mailman, even though he regularly
delivers you Benedicto Clemente's mail.

Love the weta you find on the path,
Injured by alteration.

Love the tired men, the burnt
house, the handlebars of light
on the ceiling.

Love the man on the bus who says
it all amounts to a fishing rod
or a light bulb.

Love the world of the garden.
The keyhole of bright green grass
where the stubborn palm
used to be,
bees so drunk on ginger flowers
that they think the hose water
is rain   your hair tangled in
heartsease.   Love the way,
when you come inside,
insects find their way out
from the temporary rooms of
your clothes.

JENNY BORNHOLDT

MARRIAGE MESSAGE

May your marriage bring you all the exquisite
excitement marriage should bring,
and may life grant you also patience,
tolerance, and understanding.

May you always need one another —
not so much to fill your emptiness
as to help you to know your fullness.
A mountain needs a valley to be complete;
the valley does not make
the mountain less, but more;
and the valley is more a valley because
it has a mountain towering over it.

May you need one another, but not out of weakness.
May you want one another, but not out of lack.
May you entice one another, but not compel one another.
May you embrace one another, but not encircle one another.
May you succeed in all important ways with one another,
and not fail in the little graces.
May you look for things to praise, often say, 'I love you!'
and take no notice of small faults.

If you have quarrels that push you apart,
may both of you hope to have
good sense enough to take the first step back.

May you enter into the mystery which is
the awareness of one another's
presence — no more physical than spiritual,
warm and near when you are
side by side, and warm and near when
you are in separate rooms
or even distant cities.

May you have happiness,
and may you find it making one another happy.
May you have love, and may you find it loving one another.

JAMES DILLET FREEMAN

In a long marriage there will be joy and laughter, but also sadness and sorrow, harmony and discord, as you strive to overcome adversity and fulfil your dreams.

The key value of wedlock is that it allows for intimacy between a woman and a man, who can enjoy each other's company, share ideals and expectations, confess failures and admit defeats to each other, and yet realise in union the qualities of the good life.

As you build your home, embark upon careers, and raise a family, your marriage can become a work of art in which both of you together give it line and form, colour and tone. You will be challenged every day and in every way to make your marriage work. If you do, it can become a thing of beauty, a joint creation of aesthetic splendour and enduring value.

A successful marriage is one where each partner discovers that it is better to give love than to receive it. To truly love another person is to wish that person to develop and flourish in his or her own terms.

PAUL KURTZ

Sooner or later we begin to understand
that love is more than verses on valentines
and romance in the movies.
We begin to know that love is here and now
real and true, the most important thing in our lives.
For love is the creator of our favourite memories
and the foundation of our fondest dreams.
Love is a promise that is always kept,
a fortune that can never be spent,
a seed that can flourish in even the most unlikely of places.
And this radiance that never fades, this mysterious and magical joy,
is the greatest treasure of all – one known only by those who love.

AUTHOR UNKNOWN

The key to love is understanding . . .
the ability to comprehend
not only the spoken word,
but those unspoken gestures,
the little things that say
so much by themselves.

The key to love is forgiveness . . .
to accept each other's faults
and pardon mistakes,
without forgetting,
but with remembering
what you learn from them . . .

The key to love is trust . . .
though dark doubts
lay in hollowed thoughts,
it must shine brightly on
with reassuring radiance
that suppresses fear with faith.

The key to love is sharing . . .
facing your good fortunes
as well as the bad, together;
both conquering problems —
forever searching for ways
to intensify your happiness.

The key to love is giving . . .
without thought of return,
but with the hope of just
a simple smile,
and by giving in, but never up.

The key to love is respect . . .
realising that you are
two separate people
with different ideas;
that you don't belong to each other,
but that you belong with each other
and share a mutual bond.

The key to love is inside us all . . .
it takes time and patience
to unlock all the ingredients
that will take you to its threshold;
it is a continual learning process
that demands a lot of work . . .
but the rewards are more than
worth the effort . . .

And you
are the key
to me.

ROBERT M. MILLAY

The key to happiness
Belongs to everyone on earth
Who recognises simple things
As treasures of great worth.

The changing of the seasons
The rising of the moon
Golden restful hours
On a lazy afternoon.
The music found in laughter
The beauty found in truth
The wrinkled eyes of wisdom
The innocence of youth.

Dreams the heart has woven
Letting go the cares
Reaching out and helping out
And countless answered prayers.
The loving bond of family ties
And understanding friends
The chance to make a difference
The will to make amends.
Having someone's hand to hold
The promise each day brings
The key to happiness is found
In these simple things.

EMILY MATTHEWS

Happiness in marriage is not something that just happens.

A good marriage must be created.

In marriage the little things are the big things.

It is never being too old to hold hands.

It is remembering to say 'I love you' at least once a day.

It is never going to sleep angry.

It is at no time taking the other for granted; the courtship should not end with the honeymoon, it should continue through all the years.

It is having a mutual sense of values and common objectives.

It is standing together facing the world.

It is forming a circle of love that gathers in the whole family.

It is doing things for each other, not in the attitude of duty or sacrifice, but in the spirit of joy.

It is speaking words of appreciation and demonstrating gratitude in thoughtful ways.

It is not looking for perfection in each other.

It is cultivating flexibility, patience, understanding and a sense of humour.

It is having the capacity to forgive and forget.

It is giving each other an atmosphere in which each can grow.

It is a common search for the good and the beautiful.

It is establishing a relationship in which the independence is equal, dependence is mutual and the obligation is reciprocal.

It is not only marrying the right partner, it is being the right partner.

WILFERD ARLAN PETERSON

THE FIVE FREEDOMS

The freedom to see and hear what is here,
instead of what should be, was, or will be.

The freedom to say what I feel and think,
instead of what I should.

The freedom to feel what I feel,
instead of what I ought.

The freedom to ask for what I want,
instead of always waiting for permission.

The freedom to take risks on my own behalf,
Instead of choosing to be only 'secure' and not rocking the boat.

VIRGINIA SATIR

MARRIAGE ADVICE

Let your love be stronger than your hate or anger.
Learn the wisdom of compromise, for it is better to bend a little than to break.
Believe the best rather than the worst.
People have a way of living up or down to your opinion of them.
Remember that true friendship is the basis for any lasting relationship.
The person you choose to marry is deserving of the courtesies
and kindnesses you bestow on your friends.
Please hand this down to your children and your children's children.

JANE WELLS

LOVE IS THE REASON

Love is the reason why this day
Was chosen by you both
To begin your lives together —
And love is the reason why you both
Will give with all your hearts
For the good of each other.

Love is the reason
That together you will become one —
One in hope,
One in believing in life and
One in sharing the coming years.

BRIAN ZOUCH

Chapter Eight

QUOTABLE LOVE

A short saying oft contains
much wisdom.

SOPHOCLES

Chapter Eight

A wedding speech can benefit from a quote. What bride could resist finishing her speech with Rita Rudner's quip: 'I love being married. It's so great to find that one special person you want to annoy for the rest of your life.'?

Quotations can also be used in the wedding ceremony itself. If a couple felt a special spiritual connection when they first met, the poet Rumi's quote 'Lovers don't finally meet somewhere/ They're in each other all along' would capture that special feeling.

Many civil ceremonies conclude with the celebrant or the MC proposing a toast to the couple. For example, 'Mark Twain once said "To get the full value of joy, you must have someone to divide it with." Jo and John, I wish you both that joy. Ladies and gentlemen, please raise your glasses in a toast — to Jo and John!'

Quotes can be used on wedding invitations, thank-you notes and place cards, in photograph albums, and superimposed on video footage.

Couples often choose a theme for their wedding. If the sea is a theme, the wedding stationery could read: 'As the ocean is never full of water, so is the heart never full of love.' If the sun is used as a symbol, the quote might be: 'To love and be loved is to feel the sun from both sides.' Or for a musical couple, what could be better than: 'If music be the food of love, play on.'

LOVE

As the ocean is never full of water,
so is the heart never full of love.
AUTHOR UNKNOWN

Love is, above all, the gift of oneself.
JEAN ANOUILH, *ARDÈLE*

May no gift be too small to give,
nor too simple to receive,
which is wrapped in thoughtfulness
and tied with love.
L.O. BAIRD

If you have it [love], you don't need to have anything else. If you don't have it,
it doesn't matter much what else you do have.
J.M. BARRIE

The way to love anything is to realise it might be lost.
G.K. CHESTERTON

We are all born for love . . . it is the principal existence and its only end.
BENJAMIN DISRAELI

He who is in love is wise and is becoming wiser, sees newly every time he looks
at the object beloved, drawing from it with his eyes and his mind those virtues
which it possesses.

RALPH WALDO EMERSON,'ADDRESS ON THE METHOD OF NATURE', 1841

Love is not blind — it sees more, not less. But because it sees more, it is willing
to see less.
RABBI JULIUS GORDON

Love is the great miracle cure. Loving ourselves works miracles in our lives.
LOUISE HAY, *YOU CAN HEAL YOUR LIFE*

The truth [is] that there is only one terminal dignity — love . . .
And the story of a love is not important — what is important is that one is
capable of love. It is perhaps the only glimpse we are permitted of eternity.
HELEN HAYES

Love is the master key that opens the gates of happiness.
OLIVER WENDELL HOLMES

Life is the flower for which love is the honey.
VICTOR HUGO

Life's greatest happiness is to be convinced we are loved.
VICTOR HUGO, *LES MISÉRABLES*

What a grand thing, to be loved!
What a grander thing still, to love!
VICTOR HUGO

Love is the only ecstasy, everything else weeps. To love or to have loved, that is enough. Ask nothing further. There is no other pearl to be found in the dark folds of life. To love is a consummation.
VICTOR HUGO

Love doesn't make the world go 'round.
Love is what makes the ride worthwhile.
P. JONES

Love is everything it's cracked up to be. That's why people are so cynical about it . . . It really is worth fighting for, risking everything for. And the trouble is, if you don't risk everything, you risk even more.
ERICA JONG

Love is like an eternal flame — once it is lit, it will continue to burn for all time.
KAMILA

Love doesn't just sit there, like a stone.
It has to be made like bread, remade all the time, made new.
URSULA K. LEGUIN, *LATHE OF HEAVEN*

To love is to be vulnerable.
C.S. LEWIS

The important thing was to love rather than to be loved.
W. SOMERSET MAUGHAM, *OF HUMAN BONDAGE*

Love is the triumph of imagination over intelligence.
H. L. MENCKEN

Came but for friendship,
And took away love.
THOMAS MOORE

Love is or it ain't. Thin love ain't love at all.
TONI MORRISON, *BELOVED*

Love is the extremely difficult realisation that something other than
oneself is real.
IRIS MURDOCH, *THE SUBLIME AND THE GOOD*

We can only learn to love by loving.
IRIS MURDOCH

There is always some madness in love. But there is also always some reason in
madness.
FRIEDRICH NIETZSCHE, *ON READING AND WRITING*

Love is like quicksilver in the hand. Leave the fingers open and it stays. Clutch
it, and it darts away.
DOROTHY PARKER

For one human being to love another; that is perhaps the most difficult of all
our tasks, the ultimate, the last test and proof, the work for which all other
work is but preparation.
RAINER MARIA RILKE

Love consists in this, that two solitudes protect and touch and greet each other.
RAINER MARIA RILKE

To fear love is to fear life, and those who fear life are already three parts dead.
BERTRAND RUSSELL, *MARRIAGE AND MORALS*

There is only one happiness in life, to love and be loved.
GEORGE SAND

Love comforteth like sunshine after rain.
WILLIAM SHAKESPEARE, *VENUS AND ADONIS*

Love all, trust a few. Do wrong to none.
WILLIAM SHAKESPEARE, *ALL'S WELL THAT ENDS WELL*

Love is merely madness.
WILLIAM SHAKESPEARE, *AS YOU LIKE IT*

'Tis the most tender part of love, each other to forgive.
JOHN SHEFFIELD

One word frees us of all the weight and pain of life: that word is love.
SOPHOCLES

To love is to receive a glimpse of heaven.
KAREN SUNDE

To love deeply in one direction makes us more loving in all others.
ANNE-SOPHIE SWETCHINE

Where love is, no room is too small.
TALMUD

Love is friendship set on fire.
JEREMY TAYLOR

The loving are the daring.
BAYARD TAYLOR

There is no remedy for love but to love more.
HENRY DAVID THOREAU

Love is an act of endless forgiveness, a tender look which becomes a habit.
PETER USTINOV

Time is too slow for those who wait
Too swift for those who fear
Too long for those who grieve
Too short for those who rejoice
But for those who love,
Time is eternity.
HENRY JACKSON VAN DYKE

To love and be loved is to feel the sun from both sides.
DAVID VISCOTT

Never pretend to a love which you do not actually feel, for love is not ours to command.

ALAN WATTS

To love oneself is the beginning of a lifelong romance.

OSCAR WILDE

Who, being loved, is poor?

OSCAR WILDE

LOVE IS LIKE...

Love is like a game of chess — one false move and you're mated.

AUTHOR UNKNOWN

Love is friendship set to music.

E. JOSEPH COSSMAN

Love is like pi — natural, irrational and very important.

LISA HOFFMAN

The meeting of two personalities is like the contact of two chemical substances: if there is any reaction, both are transformed.

CARL JUNG

Oh, life is a glorious cycle of song,
A medley of extemporanea;
And love is a thing that can never go wrong;
And I am Marie of Roumania.

DOROTHY PARKER

If music be the food of love, play on.

WILLIAM SHAKESPEARE, *TWELFTH NIGHT*

A love song is just a caress set to music.

SIGMUND ROMBERG

OLD LOVE

Grow old along with me, the best is yet to be.

ROBERT BROWNING

Old love rusts not.

GERMAN PROVERB

Age does not protect you from love. But love, to some extent, protects you from age.

JEANNE MOREAU

YOUNG LOVE

I pay very little regard . . . to what any young person says on the subject of marriage. If they profess a disinclination for it, I only set it down that they have not yet seen the right person.

JANE AUSTEN, *MANSFIELD PARK*

The magic of first love is our ignorance that it can ever end.

BENJAMIN DISRAELI

SOUL MATES

Henceforth there will be such
a oneness between us —
that when one weeps
the other will taste salt.

AUTHOR UNKNOWN

Don't walk in front of me, I may not follow.
Don't walk behind me, I may not lead.
Just walk beside me and be my friend forever.

ALBERT CAMUS

What greater thing is there for two human souls than to feel that they are joined together to strengthen each other in all labour, to minister to each other in all sorrow, to share with each other in all gladness, to be one with each other in the silent unspoken memories?

GEORGE ELIOT

The only gift is a portion of thyself.

RALPH WALDO EMERSON

The minute I heard my first love story,
I started looking for you, not knowing how blind that was.
Lovers don't finally meet somewhere.
They're in each other all along.

MAULANA JALALU'DDIN RUMI

Nearly all marriages, even happy ones, are mistakes: in the sense that almost certainly (in a more perfect world, or even with a little more care in this very imperfect one) both partners might be found more suitable mates. But the real soul-mate is the one you are actually married to.

J. R. R. TOLKIEN, LETTER TO MICHAEL TOLKIEN

To the world you may be one person, but to one person you may be the world.

BILL WILSON

FAMILY

But when a young lady is to be a heroine, the perverseness of forty surrounding families cannot prevent her. Something must and will happen to throw a hero in her way.

JANE AUSTEN, *NORTHANGER ABBEY*

Spread love everywhere you go:
first of all in your own home.
Give love to your children, to a wife
or husband, to a next-door neighbour.

MOTHER TERESA

MEN AND WOMEN

The enthusiasm of a woman's love is even beyond the biographer's.

JANE AUSTEN, *MANSFIELD PARK*

It is a truth universally acknowledged, that a man in possession of a large fortune must be in want of a wife.

JANE AUSTEN, *PRIDE AND PREJUDICE*

Man's best possession is a sympathetic wife.

EURIPIDES, *ANTIGONE*

A simple enough pleasure, surely, to have breakfast alone with one's husband, but how seldom married people in the midst of life achieve it.

ANNE MORROW LINDBERGH, *A GIFT FROM THE SEA*

All marriages are mixed marriages.

CHANTAL SAPERSTEIN

The best portion of a good man's life,
His little, nameless, unremembered acts,
Of kindness and of love.

WILLIAM WORDSWORTH

THE HEART

The heart has reasons that reason does not understand.

JACQUES BENIGNE BOSSUET

There is no instinct like that of the heart.

LORD BYRON

The dedicated life is the life worth living.
You must give with your whole heart.

ANNE DILLARD

Come live in my heart, and pay no rent.

SAMUEL LOVER

Now join your hands, and with your hands, your hearts.

WILLIAM SHAKESPEARE, *KING HENRY VI PART III*

MARRIAGE

Marriage has less beauty but more safety than single life. It is full of sorrows and full of joys. It lies under more burdens but it is supported by all the strengths of love. And those burdens are delightful.

A 16TH CENTURY BISHOP

What therefore God has joined together, let no man separate.

THE BIBLE, MARK 10:9

Marriage is not a ritual or an end. It is a long, intricate, intimate dance together and nothing matters more than your own sense of balance and your choice of partner.

AMY BLOOM

A good marriage is one which allows for change and growth in the individuals and in the way they express their love.

PEARL BUCK

Never say that marriage has more of joy than pain.

EURIPIDES, *ALCESTIS*

Love is an ideal thing, marriage a real thing.

GOETHE

All married couples should learn the art of battle as they should learn the art of making love. Good battle is objective and honest — never vicious or cruel. Good battle is healthy and constructive, and brings to a marriage the principle of equal partnership.

ANN LANDERS

This may seem obvious, but do marry someone you like.

MAUREEN LIPMAN, *BRIDES AND SETTING UP HOME*

A successful marriage requires falling in love many times, always with the same person.

MIGNON MCLAUGHLIN

A great marriage is not when the 'perfect couple' comes together. It is when an imperfect couple learns to enjoy their differences.

DAVE MEURER, *DAZE OF OUR WIVES*

If you would marry suitably, marry your equal.

OVID

Marriage resembles a pair of shears . . . often moving in opposite directions, yet punishing anyone that comes between them.

SYDNEY SMITH, LADY HOLLAND, *MEMOIR*

Marriage is the only adventure open to the cowardly.

VOLTAIRE

MAORI PROVERBS

He kapiti hono, he tatai hono.
That which is joined together becomes an unbroken line.

Aroha mai, aroha atu.
Love received demands love returned.

Aitia te wahine i roto i te pa harakeke.
Marry the woman in the flax bush.

E moe i tangata ringa raupa.
Marry a man with blistered hands.

He hono tangata e kore e motu; ka pa he taura waka e motu.
Marriage is permanent, unlike the mooring rope of a canoe, which is easily broken.

WIT

Among those whom I like or admire, I can find no common denominator, but among those whom I love, I can: all of them make me laugh.
W.H. AUDEN

Love is an exploding cigar we willingly smoke.
LYNDA BARRY

Love is an electric blanket with somebody else in control of the switch.
CATHY CARLYLE

There's only one way to have a happy marriage and as soon as I learn what it is I'll get married again.
CLINT EASTWOOD

I know nothing about sex because I was always married.
ZSA ZSA GABOR

Love 'em for what they are, and forgive 'em for what they ain't.
GRANDPA

Love is a snowmobile racing across the tundra and then suddenly it flips over, pinning you underneath. At night, the ice weasels come.

MATT GROENING, *LIFE IN HELL*

If love is a dream,
then marriage is the alarm clock.

JOHN HAGEE

The conception of two people living together for twenty-five years without having a cross word suggests a lack of spirit only to be admired in sheep.

ALAN PATRICK HERBERT

O Love, love, love!
Love is like a dizziness;
It winna let a poor body
Gang about his bizziness!

JAMES HOGG

I'm not a real movie star. I've still got the same wife I started out with twenty-eight years ago.

WILL ROGERS

One man's folly is another man's wife.

HELEN ROWLAND

Always get married early in the morning. That way, if it doesn't work out, you haven't wasted a whole day.

MICKEY ROONEY

Before I met my husband, I'd never fallen in love, though I'd stepped in it a few times.

RITA RUDNER

I love being married. It's so great to find that one special person you want to annoy for the rest of your life.

RITA RUDNER

I think men who have a pierced ear are better prepared for marriage. They've experienced pain and bought jewellery.

RITA RUDNER

When I meet a man I ask myself, 'Is this the man I want my children to spend their weekends with?'
RITA RUDNER

Love looks not with the eye, but with the mind,
And therefore is winged Cupid painted blind.
WILLIAM SHAKESPEARE, *A MIDSUMMER NIGHT'S DREAM*

By all means marry; if you get a good wife, you'll be happy. If you get a bad one, you'll become a philosopher.
SOCRATES

Love is the irresistible desire to be irresistibly desired.
MARK TWAIN

To get the full value of joy, you must have someone to divide it with.
MARK TWAIN

Love is an ocean of emotions, entirely surrounded by expenses.
THOMAS DEWAR

Marriage is a great institution, but I'm not ready for an institution yet.
MAE WEST

We always believe our first love is our last, and our last love is our first.
GEORGE WHYTE-MELVILLE

Index of authors

Index of first lines and titles

(titles are in italics)

ACKNOWLEDGEMENTS

Random House New Zealand and Pinky Agnew gratefully acknowledge authors, publishers, literary agents and estates as follows:

Pam Ayres and Orion Publishing Group for 'Yes I'll Marry You' (from *With These Hands*)
Robert Bell for 'Desiderata' by Max Ehrmann
Jenny Bornholdt and Victoria University Press for 'Wedding Song'
The Estate of Charles Brasch and Oxford University Press for extract from 'In Your Presence'
* Dorothy R. Colgan for 'I Promise'
Curtis Brown Ltd for 'A Word to Husbands', 'I Do, I Will, I Have', 'Tin Wedding Whistle', 'What Almost Every Woman Knows Sooner or Later'. Copyright 1962, 1949, 1941, 1934 by Ogden Nash, reprinted by permission of Curtis Brown Ltd
Egmont Books for 'We Two' by A.A. Milne (from *Now We Are Six*)
Faber and Faber for 'Foxtrot from a Play' (from *As I Walked Out One Evening* by W.H. Auden); 'Twelve Songs XII (O Tell Me the Truth about Love)' and 'Ten Songs IV (Carry Her Over the Water)' (from *Collected Shorter Poems* by W.H. Auden); 'Valentine' (from *Serious Concerns* by Wendy Cope); 'Dedication To My Wife' (from *Collected Poems 1909-1962* by T.S. Eliot); 'Scaffolding' (from *Death of a Naturalist* by Seamus Heaney); 'The Confirmation' (from *Collected Poems* by Edwin Muir)
* The late James Dillet Freeman for 'Marriage Message'
Ruth Gilbert for 'Not Made With Hands' and 'Even in the Dark'
Pia Glover and the Denis Glover Estate for 'About Ourselves'
Dinah Hawken and Victoria University Press for 'The Settlement'
Heacock Literary Agency and Souvenir Press for permission to print a shortened version of 'The Art of Marriage' by Wilferd Arlan Peterson, which was published earlier in *The New Book of the Art of Living*
* The late Adrian Henri for 'Without You' from *Collected Poems*
Henry Holt and Company for 'The Master Speed' from *The Poetry of Robert Frost* edited by Edward Connery Lathem. Copyright 1936 by Robert Frost, copyright 1964 by Lesley Frost Ballantine, copyright 1969 by Henry Holt and Company. Reprinted by permission of Henry Holt and Company, LLC
Keri Hulme and Auckland University Press for extract from 'Winesong 15'

Kevin Ireland for 'Inventing You'

Roger McGough for 'Ten Milk Bottles' and 'Epic Film' (from *Summer with Monika*), reprinted by permission of PFD on behalf of Roger McGough. Copyright 1967 Roger McGough.

Rod McKuen for 'Taking the Time' (from *Seasons in the Sun*)

Emily Matthews for 'The Key to Happiness'

Yair Mazor for the translation of 'A Poem of Bliss' by Ronny Someck

Robert Millay for 'The Keys to Love'

NAACP — the publisher wishes to thank the National Association for the Advancement of Colored People for authorising the use of Dorothy Parker's works 'One Perfect Rose' and 'Comment' ('Oh, life is a glorious cycle of song', page 177)

Edmund O'Neill for 'Marriage Joins Two People in the Circle of its Love'

The Penguin Group for 'Valentine' by Carol Ann Duffy (from *I Wouldn't Thank You For A Valentine*) and 'All the While' (from *Collected Poems 1953–1993* by John Updike)

Terri McPherson for extract from 'Soulmates by Choice' (from www.wisehearts.com)

Marge Piercy for 'The Chuppah' (from *My Mother's Body*)

Hugh Prather for 'Today I Will Marry My Best Friend'

Ten Speed Press for 'The Five Freedoms', reprinted by permission from *Making Contact* by Virginia Satir. Copyright 1976 by Virginia Satir, Celestial Arts, a division of Ten Speed Press, Berkeley, CA, www.tenspeed.com.

Brian Turner and McIndoe Publishers for 'Like Lamplight'

Jane Wells for 'Marriage Advice'

Whiteknights Press and The University of Reading for 'Acknowledgement' by A. S. J. Tessimond, from *The Collected Poems of A. S. J. Tessimond, with translations from Jacques Prevert*, ed. Hubert Nicholson (Whiteknights Press, Reading, 1985)

Time Warner Book Group for 'Variation on the Word *Sleep*' (from *Eating Fire: Selected Poems 1965–1995* by Margaret Atwood)

Brian Zouch for 'Love is the Reason' and 'This Day'

* Every effort was made to contact these authors or their representatives, but without success.